I0147950

DYING TO MEET YOU

CONFESSIONS OF A FUNERAL DIRECTOR

ANGJOLIE MEI

Microcosm Publishing

Portland, Ore | Cleveland, Ohio

DYING TO MEET YOU: Confessions of A Funeral Director

© Angjolie Mei, 2020, 2025
Original English edition published by Epigram Books Pte Ltd (Singapore)
hello@epigram.sg / www.epigrambooks.sg
© This edition Microcosm Publishing 2025 available in the U.S., Canada, UK, and Oceania only
First edition – 3,000 copies – September 2, 2025
ISBN 9781648414381
This is Microcosm #1000

Some names and identifying details have been changed to protect the privacy of individuals.
Cover by Lindsey Cleworth
American edition edited by Sarah Koch
Design by Sarah Koch and Joe Biel

To join the ranks of high-class stores that feature Microcosm titles, talk to your rep: In the U.S. COMO (Atlantic), ABRAHAM (Midwest), BOB BARNETT (Texas, Oklahoma, Arkansas, Louisiana), IMPRINT (Pacific), TURNAROUND (UK), UTP/MANDA (Canada), NEWSOUTH (Australia/New Zealand), Observatoire (Africa, Europe), IPR (Middle East), APD (Asia), HarperCollins (India), and FAIRE in the gift trade.

For a catalog, write or visit:
Microcosm Publishing
2752 N Williams Ave.
Portland, OR 97227

All the news that's fit to print at www.Microcosm.Pub/Newsletter

Get more copies of this book at www.Microcosm.Pub/DyingtoMeetYou

EU Safety Information: https://microcosmpublishing.com/gpsr

For more arcane books, visit www.Microcosm.Pub/Witchy

Microcosm's workers and authors are paid solely from book sales. If you downloaded this book from some sketchy part of the Internet or picked up what appears to be a bootleg, please support our hardworking team by purchasing a copy directly from us and encouraging your communities to do the same. An MIT study revealed that AI inhibits humanity's critical thinking ability. Since critical thinking is one of our core values, we prohibit any use of our books to "train" generative artificial "intelligence" (AI) technologies, because seriously, WTF.

MICROCOSM PUBLISHING is Portland's most diversified publishing house and distributor, with a focus on the colorful, authentic, and empowering. Our books and zines have put your power in your hands since 1996, equipping readers to make positive changes in their lives and in the world around them. Microcosm emphasizes skill-building, showing hidden histories, and fostering creativity through challenging conventional publishing wisdom with books and bookettes about DIY skills, food, bicycling, gender, self-care, and social justice. What was once a distro and record label started by Joe Biel in a drafty bedroom was determined to be *Publishers Weekly*'s fastest-growing publisher of 2022 and #3 in 2023 and 2024, and is now among the oldest independent publishing houses in Portland, OR, and Cleveland, OH. We are a politically moderate, centrist publisher in a world that has inched to the right for the past 80 years.

Did you know that you can buy our books directly from us at sliding scale rates? Support a small, independent publisher and pay less than Amazon's price at **www.Microcosm.Pub.**

Global labor conditions are bad, and our roots in industrial Cleveland in the '70s and '80s made us appreciate the need to treat workers right. Therefore, our books are MADE IN THE USA.

*For all who have lost a loved one—may you find
solace in insight and wisdom.*

Contents

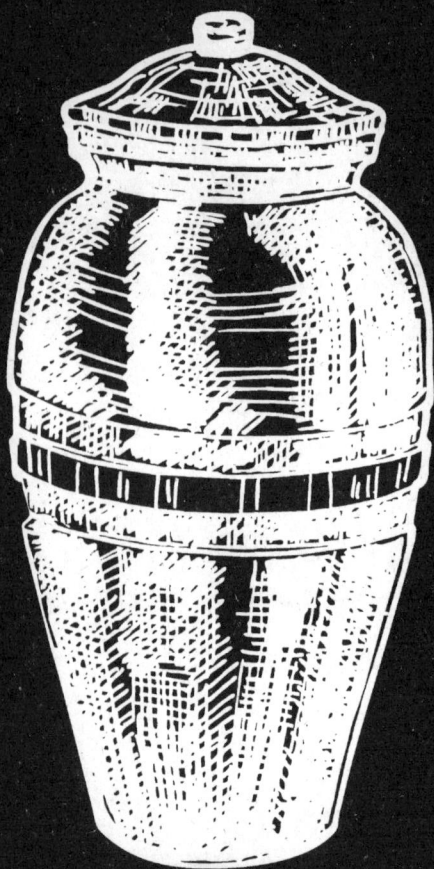

Introduction

"Many of my clients are dying to meet me." That's the clue I offer to strangers who ask me what I do for a living. Another one-liner that I sometimes throw out to break the ice is: I have the best clients in the world because they never complain.

I'm a funeral director. Some might think it's bad luck to associate with someone of my profession, but the fact is that everyone will eventually need the kind of services I provide.

The number of deaths in Singapore has been on the rise since 1960 and will not go down any time soon, given the country's aging population. About 20,000 Singaporeans died in 2019, and the numbers have been on a slow but steady upward trend to 26,888 in 2023.

I have written this book, in part, because I want to lift the shroud of mystery that surrounds death in Singapore. There are misconceptions and ambiguity aplenty, but also a lot of curiosity about the topic.

When I take part in panel discussions as part of seminars, forums, and talks, I am usually hit with a barrage of questions from the floor. People want to know what funeral directors do with the bodies of the dead, what to do when their loved ones die, and how the living should prepare for death. They are innately fascinated with death because it is not something encountered every day.

I also want to dispel stereotypes. Funeral directors—popularly called morticians—are a favorite feature in horror stories, and they are usually pale, grim, cadaverous men. In the past, when one thought of funeral directors in Singapore, the image that came to mind would

be that of a Hokkien-speaking[1], chain-smoking middle-aged man in a singlet, who had ended up in what was thought of as a dead-end, *pantang* (inauspicious) job no one else wanted.

But funeral services have evolved over time, from largely ritualistic ceremonies to meaningful, carefully curated events. In essence, funeral directors are event planners. The nitty-gritty of what I do starts when I get a call from a client whose family member has died. I help the family organize the entire funeral event—from making sure the body looks presentable and acceptable to booking the venue for the wake and organizing it, and helping family members pick out their loved one's cremains (cremated remains) after a funeral, right until their loved one is settled in their final resting place.

People often ask me why I chose to become a funeral director. I love my job. I view every funeral I do as a celebration of someone's life. As we rejoice whenever babies are born, we should celebrate when people have completed their life journeys—remember the things they have done, the people they have touched, and the differences they have made. After all, a funeral is like life's graduation ceremony; it is so very important. A funeral is not a day in a lifetime. It is a lifetime in a day.

---

1 A Southern Chinese dialect that is sometimes associated with a more gruff, working-class identity.

I am one of a handful of certified funeral directors in Singapore—of which only a very small proportion are women—and the only certified funeral celebrant, which means that I am trained to organize funerals that reflect the personality and life story of the deceased. The religion of the dead and their families also determines how a funeral is conducted. Apart from Hindu and Muslim funerals, I have organized funerals for Christians, Catholics, Buddhists, Taoists, Soka practitioners, and freethinkers. In recent years, we have observed many funerals of mixed religions, such as a Muslim–Buddhist funeral we had not long ago. There was an imam and a Buddhist monk at the funeral wake at the same time; at the end of the three-day wake, Buddhist rituals were conducted for the deceased, who was then buried in a Muslim cemetery. So as you see, my job is incredibly fulfilling—one in which I have learned many life lessons through the funerals I have organized, and from the interesting people I have met.

Becoming a funeral director as part of my own life journey is a tale in itself. I never set out to become one. What I always say, when asked about my choice of profession, is that "I didn't choose funeral directing. Funeral directing chose me." As a child, I was scarred by encounters with death. But when my father, Ang Yew Seng, a pioneer in the Singapore funeral industry, died in 2004, I had to quit my job and support my mother in a male-dominated industry.

It is also fitting that a funeral director who talks all day long about remembrance should write her own biography, perhaps to distribute at her own funeral one day.

As you read this book about my life as a funeral director, you will unavoidably think about death. But also, think about your life—make it count and make it last. Because I hope I will not have to meet you for a long time yet.

I Am Ang Yew Seng's Daughter

*M*y mother is a funeral director. My younger sister, Sarah, is an embalmer and she is married to a funeral director. My older sister, a trained accountant, manages the accounts for both my business and my mother's. Aside from my brother, who is in between jobs, nearly my entire family works in the funeral industry.

At Sarah's wedding in 2015, probably half of those from Singapore's funeral industry were present. Many of the guests, chain-smokers who work in the business, flooded the toilet for their smoke breaks, drawing the ire of the hotel manager who threatened to call the fire department upon witnessing the clouds of smoke coming from the bathroom.

While we make a living off death—and we do have a tendency to pore over obituaries—ours is a normal, happy four-generation family with plenty of babies and children to play with at our social gatherings. We don't usually talk about work. At most, we exclaim over coincidences, like when I discovered that my company had embalmed my mother's former teacher and organized her funeral. Or if someone I knew had died and I found out via our family WhatsApp group chat that my mother or brother-in-law was taking up the case, I might ask them to give a goodwill discount. My sister, when she was pregnant, was also "allowed" by our family to continue her embalming work well into her third trimester despite the superstition that expectant women should keep away from the dead. Her husband, mother, and sister all needed her skills. Likewise, when I was pregnant, my family had no objections to my conducting funerals and seminars up till one week before my expected due date.

My siblings and I would likely have ended up in "normal" salaried professions—perhaps in office-bound jobs, sales, or marketing—had it not been for my father, Ang Yew Seng. He was the second in a family of 10 children born to immigrants from China. In post-war Singapore, families were typically large, and children were not pampered or nurtured. My father, like most children in working-class families then, didn't stay long in school because he had to work to help feed his siblings. At 12, he started doing odd jobs, like selling bee hoon[2] as a street hawker.

Fortuitously, his uncle, who had migrated from China, started a funeral business. My father decided to join him in the trade at a young age, making caskets by hand. In those days, when Singapore had enough land for people to be buried rather than cremated, the heavy caskets were painstakingly fashioned from actual tree wood. The tools he used are still kept in the family.

In the 1970s, the government, realizing that the dead were taking up space in land-scarce Singapore, started to clear cemeteries and redevelop the land by constructing roads and buildings. The biggest cemetery landowners at the time were

2 A rice vermicelli noodle beloved throughout Southeast Asia.

the Chinese clan associations, who altogether owned over 1,000 acres of land.

The Chinese had to quickly get used to the idea of cremation. At the time, the Hindus were already cremating their dead. Muslims did not, as the practice is forbidden in Islam. Cremation, however, caught on amongst the Buddhists and Christians who, up till then, had mostly buried their dead.

Cremation called for a different sort of casket from those used in burials. It had to be light, and it had to burn easily. My father was then an active volunteer at the Bright Hill Temple, also known as the Kong Meng San Phor Kark See Monastery. The Reverend there suggested that he create thinner, lighter caskets with traditional motifs, such as lotus flowers and Buddhist swastikas, so Buddhists might find it easier to support the idea of cremation. In response, my father produced these caskets and started his business, Ang Yew Seng Cremation and Undertaker, which was located at Thomson Road. The Reverend directed the temple devotees to my father to organize the funerals of their family members, and his business took off. He moved to Sin Ming Drive in 1984 when the Singapore government took back the land where his first office was located, and the company's name was changed to Ang Yew Seng Funeral Parlor.

Pa, who was tall and lean, cut a suave presence in the funeral industry. Back in the day, he stood out in a sea of Bermuda shorts and slipper-clad funeral workers as he always insisted on being properly dressed in a formal button-down shirt or a neat polo shirt. He wore sunglasses because he wanted to look good, and because he had cataracts and wanted to protect his eyes. The sunglasses became part of his corporate image. It was so much a part of his identity that we placed them in his casket after he had passed away.

While my father was street-smart, he wasn't what you would have called a paragon of virtue. He had once been arrested for allegedly murdering a cashier in 1962, although he was later acquitted. Throughout his life, he was a gambler and a heavy drinker. He regularly imbibed Martell from a glass neat. Luckily, his business star shone bright and he was always able to fund his vices. Publicly, he was better known as a philanthropist of sorts. He provided many free funerals to the poor and needy in the Chinese Buddhist community. That earned him the title of "The Coffin King."

His work occupied him 24/7, as people die at any time of the day. Funeral directors don't enjoy regular working hours. The dead saw a lot more of him than we did at home. He worked hard to ensure that his family was well provided for, and his hours were long and erratic. He came home when we were already asleep, sometimes as late as 3 am, and he would still be sleeping when we left for school the next day. He was so preoccupied with his work that he was mostly oblivious to his family.

Once, when my elder sister was 12, he was asked, "How old is your daughter?"

"Oh, she is 16," he replied, glancing up at my sister, who was tall for her age.

He placed no importance on birthday celebrations—not even his own. We once organized a surprise dinner for him, luring him to the restaurant on the pretext that he was having dinner with my mother's relatives. When we brought out the cake and sang "Happy Birthday" to him, he looked around in confusion before whipping out his wallet to check the birth date on his identity card.

As someone who had dealt with death his entire working life, my father was surprisingly not better equipped to meet it than everyone else. He did not make any provisions for death— he did not prepare his family for after his death, and he did not specify the kind of funeral he wanted. Perhaps he had not imagined that he would be dying quite so soon.

Pa died of renal failure after a failed operation in February 2004, further complicated by the fact that he had been diagnosed with stage four colon cancer in late 2003.

Prior to his diagnosis, we did not see much of him as he was busy with work all the time, but during those last few months of his life, I grew much closer to him. I looked after him, changed his colostomy bag in the wake of his colon removal, and chauffeured him to his medical appointments as he was too weak to drive. At that time, I was working in my first job as a management trainee in a logistics company.

He wanted people to remember him as he was when he was healthy; he did not like people to see him in his sickened state. Very few were allowed near him. From being the emotionally distant, capable breadwinner of the house, he became someone who depended on me and the rest of his family.

One of the last happy memories we had of him was at our traditional Chinese New Year reunion dinner that took place 18 days before he died. It was bittersweet because it was the first and, though we did not know it then, the last time our family would be enjoying the reunion dinner together. In the past, he had always been too busy to join us for the duration of the entire meal.

As he wanted to avoid being seen by relatives, the steamboat dinner was held at our home instead of my grandmother's. Instead of the noisy gathering of multiple families crowding into one flat, it was just the six of us—my father, mother, three siblings, and me. The food was simple and Pa, who rarely ate sweet things, made a special request for my mother's homemade jelly. It was the best Chinese New Year reunion dinner I had ever had because for the first time, Pa did not have to rush off to work. Little did I expect that this first time would be our last.

About two weeks later, he had what was meant to be a minor operation to close his stoma—an artificial opening in his skin that had been created to allow feces to pass through—but because of complications, the procedure ended up taking eight hours. His kidneys failed and his blood pressure plunged over the next three days. As his condition rapidly deteriorated, the doctors quickly summoned my family—I still remember it was on 7 February 2004 at 8 am—and we rushed down to the Singapore General Hospital. We were delayed by rigorous temperature checks—that was the year SARS had hit Singapore—before we saw him in the chilly intensive care unit. There were no chairs in his room, as the ICU is not a place for visitors to linger. All of us crowded around his bed, which was heated for his comfort.

When he saw my mother, he didn't say a word, but he raised his fist, lifted his second finger and curled it downward—a gesture that symbolizes death. He knew that he was dying, and he realized that there were matters he had left unattended. In the last few hours they spent together, before he became unresponsive, Ma and Pa discussed his debts. They thought I didn't understand as they spoke in Hokkien, but I knew that he owed people money.

Pa also wanted to see his only son and youngest child. Up until then, we had not brought my nine-year-old brother Zachary to the hospital because of fears over SARS. When Zachary arrived, he was bewildered to see us all crying as he did not understand what was happening. In all his naivety, he asked, "When can we go home?" We bade him to hold Pa's hand, and Pa silently clasped back in response, his eyes shut as life slipped away.

Pa's blood pressure dropped throughout the day. Gradually, he slipped into a deep slumber. Sometimes he would hum a tune, although I could not figure out what he was humming. I kept telling him, "Let's go home, Pa. You will get better and let us go home." I was still in denial of the fact that my Pa, the patriarch, the breadwinner of my family, was slowly slipping away from this realm. When his heart rate fell sharply to about 30 beats per minute in the evening, I was alone with him as the rest of my family had just stepped out to rest on the chairs outside the ICU ward. I quickly rushed out to the nursing station and asked the nurses, "Is my father dying?" They replied nonchalantly, "Yes, he is."

I desperately herded the rest of my family back into the room to say goodbye. Because of what I had heard Pa and Ma talking about earlier, I assured Pa, "I will take care of the family. You do not need to worry, Pa." He died that day at 8 pm, 12 hours after the doctors had first gathered us together.

As I gently stroked his arm, I realized that his was the first dead body I had ever touched. He was still warm. Then, even though his heart had stopped beating, a tear slipped from under his closed eyelid. I was still in disbelief that he had left us at age 64. I was not ready to bid him farewell. I was wailing so loudly in the ward; I kept asking my Pa to go home with us and not leave us. I started bargaining with him—I will take care of the family if he woke up. He still had to watch me get married. I realize that when we lose someone who is dear to us, it is never an easy process to go through, as we experience different stages of grief. I kept holding on to his hand; I did not want to forget the feeling.

It also felt completely natural for me to continue talking to him, telling him to rest in peace. Even though he had passed away, I still wanted to tell him so many things that I wished I had told him before. It was only later in the course of my work as a funeral director that I found out that a person's hearing is the last of the senses to go in the dying process, which is why we should continue talking to our loved ones when they are on their deathbed, even if they are unconscious or unable to respond.

Apart from coping with the grief of losing my father, I was also dealing with the fallout from a breakup with a man whom I was to have married on the 6th of February 2004, the day before Pa died. My ex-fiancé was four years older than I was, and I had dreamt of getting married and giving my parents grandchildren. I had chosen to overlook the fact that he often dictated many aspects of my life, including enforcing a curfew, and that in the four years we were dating he had only deigned to meet my father twice.

My mother had often asked if I was sure he was the one for me. But it was Pa's sickness that forced me to see the light. The moment I found out that Pa's surgery would take place just a day before our ceremony at the Registry of Marriages, I called my then-boyfriend.

"My dad needs to go through a crucial surgery the day before our marriage registration. We need to postpone the wedding."

My ex-fiancé coldly responded, "It's me, and not you, who gets to decide if the wedding will be postponed." In what would be my first act of defiance against him during the entire four years we had been dating, I retorted, "I don't care!" and hung up the phone. Subsequently, in my second and final act of defiance, I called off the wedding and ended our relationship.

The emotional stress from the breakup and Pa's death caused my weight to plunge. I lost 22 lbs within two months.

When Pa's body was brought back to his own funeral parlor, his friends and long-time colleagues, who had weathered the industry with him for decades, broke down and cried. The usual embalmer, one of Pa's buddies, could not bring himself to perform his task. It had to be outsourced to a third party, and she did a wonderful job.

Pa's funeral was organized by my mother. She had been helping him in his business and was in the best position to do so. His friends and colleagues also made sure that the man for whom they had the greatest respect had a send-off worthy of a veteran funeral director. Pa's wake lasted seven days, which is considered relatively long and is usually for those who have a multitude of family and friends wanting to say goodbye.

Because of Pa's lifelong work with the Buddhist temple, many monks from Myanmar, Sri Lanka, and Thailand came to chant prayers throughout the funeral. Donations were received from far-flung Buddhist temples, including one from Sri Lanka.

His funeral and cremation were held on the 13th of February 2004. All the funeral directors who ran their businesses along Sin Ming Drive gathered to say goodbye to one of their own.

The day after the funeral, my siblings, Ma, and I all went together to collect Pa's remains. As we picked his cremains from the tray with chopsticks and placed them into an urn, Ma joked, "Your dad never bought me flowers or chocolates on Valentine's Day. The first gift he gave me was his cremains."

The end of my father's life would mark the start of my "accidental" career. That was also my first official day in the funeral industry. I had to support my mother. There were debts to be repaid and a business to run. If Pa had known I was joining the business, I imagine he would have reacted the same way he had when I had taken over the wheel of his beloved car for the first time.

I had asked him then, "Pa, may I drive your car?"

He hesitated, unwilling to let go of the wheel, unsure if I would be able to handle the large Jaguar. But, aware that he was too ill to drive, he relented. Thereafter, I did all the driving.

Even now, 16 years after his death, I still soar on my father's reputation. Old hands in the funeral industry still know me as "*Ang Yew Seng eh za bor gia*"—"Ang Yew Seng's daughter" in Hokkien—which compels them to trust me and work with me.

Some people resent being known as so-and-so's child. They struggle with the patriarchal legacy. Do I mind riding on my father's coat-tails? To me, it is an honor—I am proud to be Ang Yew Seng's daughter.

Chapter 2

A Man's World

T was having dinner with nine men, in their forties and fifties, at a restaurant in Vietnam. There were only two ladies present—me and the quiet wife of one of the men. At 29, I was quite a bit younger than my companions.

Dinner conversation—painstakingly conducted through interpreters—centered around plans to transform a plot of land in Vietnam into a memorial garden where people could go to pay respects to their loved ones. I was there as one of four partners of TransLifeCare, a funeral consultancy that I had started in 2010 with three men: a Canadian embalmer, a Malaysian funeral home and memorial garden owner, and a Filipino owner of over 20 funeral homes. Outside of Singapore, there aren't many women in the industry either. I was accompanied by the Canadian at the dinner as my other partners had not yet arrived in Vietnam. Our aim was to sell our ideas to the landowner, a Vietnamese military general, and to try to get the job.

The XO cognac flowed freely and I made sure I sipped very slowly, the alcohol burning its way down my throat, as I wanted to remain lucid. I even had to secretly inform the waitress to pour tea into my shot glass instead of XO cognac, hoping that the General did not notice. After dinner, the General announced in Vietnamese, "Let's continue in the hotel room." The party moved on to a suite, my Canadian business partner's room, where the drinking and merrymaking continued.

In the room full of intoxicated men, I was nervous. The General, who had been making me increasingly uncomfortable as he intruded into my private space, kept getting closer and attempting to get me to drink more, but I remained careful and sober. When the doorbell rang, I quickly took the opportunity to stand up and open the door, hoping to get away from the General. The moment I did so, a pair of steely arms wrapped around my waist. It was the General, who had followed closely behind me. From the corner of my eye, I saw him reach out, swipe my room key card which I had carelessly left on the table, and pass it to one of his minions, who was standing at the door. Reluctantly, the minion took my room card, walked to the next room and opened my room door. This man, who had been liaising with me for the past few days, did not dare to look me in the eye. He was afraid to defy his boss and he was also embarrassed at his boss' behavior. The General, who was much stronger than I was, lifted me up—my feet could barely touch the ground—and walked into my room. I yelled in English, to no avail, "Please don't do this!" He didn't understand what I said, although I was sure he understood my tone.

He tossed me onto the bed and my mind went blank. The door clicked shut. I prayed, very hard. A second later, his phone suddenly rang. Even more fortuitously, he stepped out of my room to answer his call. Seizing the opportunity, I fled straight back to where my Canadian partner was still drinking away, oblivious to what had happened. I slapped him on his arm and yelled, "I'm not doing this deal anymore!" The tension and adrenaline that had earlier flooded my body suddenly drained and, like a pricked balloon, I felt deflated. As I sobbed, the interpreter, chastened, came to me and offered his apologies. I reckoned this was probably not the first time such a situation had occurred, and he had to apologize on behalf of his boss.

What the phone call the General had received was about I will never know, and he left without a backward glance after his conversation. The incident was, to me, a sobering reminder that the funeral industry is one where a woman is a rarity and is often not respected.

There are many industries in which women form the minority, such as engineering, aviation, and law enforcement. It is never easy for the first few women who enter such professions. In March 2020, I read in the newspapers about Ms. Sapna Jhangiani, the first woman lawyer in Singapore to be made Queen's Counsel in England. It is perhaps even harder in the funeral industry. Most Asians associate death with bad luck. Most men would not want to marry women who are tainted with death. Even without the superstition, it is a demanding job. The wife of a funeral director once told me that whenever they went out together, whether it was for a dinner, movie, or family gathering, her husband would have to leave when he received a call from a potential client. She would wait for him in the car until he was done with the funeral arrangements. He was passionate about his job; he joined the industry when he was only 18 as he had to take over from his funeral director father who had died suddenly. Sadly, he suffered the same fate as his father when he was in his thirties, following a car accident, leaving behind his wife and a young child.

For those working in the funeral industry, there are no fixed working hours. Work-life balance? Time with children? Forget it.

My mother would have led a very different life had she married anyone other than a funeral director. After her wedding, her friends shunned her. They imagined an aura of death about her, and that it would rub off on them if they associated with her. In another life, she would also never have had to venture into the industry and put up with the discrimination against her gender there, and struggle to hold the fort after my father died.

But fate had put her firmly in my father's path. His favorite coffee shop, which was just next to his funeral shop premises, was owned by her parents. Ma used to help out there after school, doling out coffee, kaya toast, and nasi lemak while still clad in her school uniform. My father must have seemed like a bit of an "uncle" to her at first as he was a good 15 years older than she was.

When she first met him, Pa was still a bachelor. Attempts by his family to matchmake him in the past had failed. Most women would not want to marry a man who touched dead bodies all day.

My mother was young, but she knew her heart. She fell in love with Pa despite his job, and he fell in love with her. They started dating, and they made quite a sight when he chauffeured her to school in his Subaru red sports car. Her schoolmates gossiped and whispered about her. Her family was reluctant about the match at first, as Pa's age and occupation made him an unorthodox boyfriend. But they soon warmed up to him, as he was always respectful and deferential to them, particularly to the older members of the family.

They got married in 1977, when she was 22 and he was 37. They were in a hurry to marry, not for any dishonorable reason, but because her paternal grandmother had died that year and Chinese tradition dictates that if a direct family member dies, any wedding must take place within 100 days, or the couple would have to wait for three years. My parents' Buddhist wedding ceremony was conducted at Kong Meng San Phor Kark See Monastery (known to many as Bright Hill Temple), and it was an open house wedding as my father had had a public invitation printed in the newspapers. The wedding was also reported in the media. People were invited to walk in, grab a plate, sit at a table, and feast on the vegetarian wedding spread.

It was a happy occasion that marked a high point in my mother's life. But she had sacrificed a university education to become a housewife and mother at the age of 24, a choice that haunted her later in her life when my father died and she had to support the family with few skills. My father was somewhat of a chauvinist. He wanted to provide for his wife and did not think she should have to work. When she tried starting a home business selling agar-agar to make some extra money, he put his foot down.

She only started wading into the funeral business when Pa's assistant stopped turning up for work and he needed one urgently. I was then already 15, and Ma was pregnant with her fourth child. Sporting a swollen belly, she answered the phones and managed the accounts. She later graduated to handling funeral arrangements.

Becoming a funeral director was never my ambition, and I am certain my parents never wanted me to become one. My father never shared any inspiring stories about the differences he had made in people's lives through his work and I never grew up hanging around the funeral parlor, despite what most people might think. The fact was, my father never asked any of us to come to his shop on weekends to help out. It could well be because we were female. In fact, I had wanted to be an engineer when I grew up because there were many on my mum's side of the family. Additionally, it was a common belief in Singapore that a career in engineering guaranteed an iron rice bowl[3].

---

3 A common Chinese idiom referring to an occupation that has high job security.

Until I was four, when we moved into a flat in Ang Mo Kio, I had enjoyed an idyllic childhood growing up in one of the last *kampongs*, or villages, in Singapore. Our house had walls made of wooden boards, a rickety zinc roof, and stood on stilts. A couple of rabbits and chickens ran around the compound. By then, most kampongs had been phased out in favor of HDB estates[4] with high-rise flats. My kampong, called Dua Chiu Ka ("big tree" in Hokkien), was in the area that is now Jalan Pemimpin.

Privacy in the kampong house consisted of rooms divided by curtains; plastic bags, rags, and various odds and ends hung from hooks placed willy-nilly all over the walls of the house. Instead of using taps with running water, we washed our hands with water from a large wooden tub at the back of the house. I loved dipping my hands into the tub and playing with the water until my skin was all wrinkled. That was often where I could be found every day.

Thereafter, once we moved into an HDB flat, I enjoyed a typical Singaporean childhood filled with a glorious assortment of enrichment classes on which my mother spared no expense—I learned art, drawing, piano, dancing, cooking, computers, wushu, calligraphy, swimming, and even trained to be a lifeguard at a tender age.

Following an academic career that blossomed slowly (kindergarten: zero for spelling; junior college: grades A, B, and B), I ended up at the National University of Singapore's Faculty of Arts and Social Sciences, where I graduated in 2002 with majors in psychology and economics. I then joined a logistics firm as a management trainee. Until then, my life was hardly different from that of any other young Singaporean.

But everything changed when my father died in 2004. We were always under the illusion that this security blanket would

---

4 Standing for Housing and Development Board, these are public housing complexes in Singapore that range from low to upper-middle class housing and are often characterized by a tight knit community with shops, cafes, and communal spaces such as "void decks," where events, parties, weddings, or funerals are sometimes held.

stay on forever. When he was alive, the dollars flowed freely. Any time we needed money, he would peel the notes off a thick stack of fifties that he carried with him like a typical Chinese *towkay*, or business owner. He did not have any ATM or credit cards.

But when he died, we discovered that he had left behind only $8,752 in his estate. He had not bought any insurance policies in the event of his death. He had never considered a succession plan for his business. He also owed his creditors a six-figure sum from gambling, including some debts incurred from betting on the 2002 World Cup results. I once overheard him checking his bet over the phone. He asked his friend, "Which color are we betting on?" He did not even know which team he was placing his wager on—he had differentiated the teams by the colors of their kits. He was even gambling shortly before his death in an attempt to make money to pay off his earlier debts. In my eyes, his weakness for gambling was his one failing. He was otherwise a loving husband and father, and a good provider. But his debts left his wife, three daughters, and young son in dire straits. My eldest sister had landed a well-paying job as an accountant with one of the Big Four firms and was on her way to becoming a certified public accountant, but my younger sister and brother were still in school.

So it was left to my mother and me, whether we liked it or not, to keep the business going—two women, one past her prime, the other just starting out in her professional life, in an industry that was unfriendly towards women. Ma used to tell me, "A woman has to be able to depend on herself, and not on her husband." That was the lesson she had learnt the hard way. I saw her strength as a woman come to the fore when she organized my father's funeral. It was not easy for her, but at that point she had been helping out in the office with sales and meeting clients, and his employees knew she was the Lady Boss who would take over the business.

A few hours before my father was due to be cremated, my mother had to meet with a bereaved couple. The meeting room was filled with our relatives who were there for my father's funeral. They quietly filed out of the room and left Ma and me to talk business with the couple, who were planning the funeral of the family's matriarch. That was the first time I sat in to listen to a funeral arrangement. It was my first on-job training. Ma went through the motions of the meeting. But halfway through, her voice broke and she started to sob. The couple, aware that the owner of the funeral parlor was being cremated that day and that Ma was his wife, were sympathetic. Ma wiped her tears away and stoically continued with the discussion. That day, I learned that our emotions should not override our professionalism.

After my father's funeral, we had to give up his Jaguar, which was costing over $3,000 a month in installments and maintenance. I was prepared to dive into what my father had been doing for decades. Right after my father's funeral, I quit my job at the logistics firm where I had been working for about one and a half years, and joined my mother to run the funeral business. The challenges began immediately. Rumors had been circulating among those in the industry that my father's business could not function without him, and that Ang Yew Seng Funeral Parlor had closed down. We had to prove the naysayers wrong. We made sure we turned up at the wakes and funerals we organized to literally "show face" and make our presence felt so the guests would know that the Ang Yew Seng Funeral Parlor brand was still going strong.

We knew we had to work hard to keep the business afloat. One night, Ma received a call from a man whose father had died, and who was looking for a funeral director. We hurriedly drove straight to the Singapore General Hospital.

We were met with a scene that is fairly typical when someone dies—droves of family members clustered outside the hospital ward, some sobbing, some grieving silently. The old man who had passed away had six children. The one who had contacted us was the youngest son, a peace-loving Buddhist who unfortunately was not the only decision-maker. The main decision-maker turned out to be his eldest brother, a stocky bull of a man in his fifties who was as overbearing as he was stout.

Ma gathered the family members who were there, intending to walk through the funeral arrangements that needed to be made. When she tried to get everyone to sit down in a quiet corner, the eldest brother snapped at her in Hokkien, "Don't speak any further. We will wait for the rest of the family to arrive first."

His arms were crossed and he gave her plenty of side-eye. The overwhelming impression we had of him was that he was sneering at us, that he despised us for preying on his family in their time of grief, and that he did not want to work with us as he did not think two women could do the job of planning his father's funeral well enough.

Ma patiently and quietly sat in the corner. I was livid when I saw how my mother had been disrespectfully shoved aside. My barely restrained fury must have been apparent. The man who had first called us apologized: "I'm sorry. My brother is just like that."

At that moment, the decision-maker looked at us from across the room as we sat on the couch and asked brusquely, in the Hokkien dialect, *"Lin toh lou lai e?"* ("Which company are you from?")

Ma replied, *"Wa lang si* Ang Yew Seng." ("We are from Ang Yew Seng.") At this, he stopped frowning and raised his eyebrows in surprise.

"Li si Ang Yew Seng *e simi lang?"* ("How are you related to Ang Yew Seng?")

"Wa si i e char bor lang, ji si i e char bo kia." ("I'm his wife, and this is his daughter.")

Those were the words that worked in our favor. With a 180-degree change in attitude, he immediately walked over and extended his hand. Ma had the presence of mind to respond with hers despite the earlier hostility she had received from him. As he gripped her hand in a firm handshake, he looked at her and said, *"Wa bat lu e ang. I si ho lang."* ("I knew your husband. He was a good man.")

The deal was closed quickly and we organized the funeral for the family.

While Pa's name could have carried us for a few more years, I was not content to merely continue where he had left off. My mother has often chastised me for being so driven by ambition, but I make no apologies for it. I was determined to spread my wings in the funeral industry.

There were four veteran funeral workers who had worked for my father for decades, whom we affectionately called the Four Heavenly Kings, echoing the nickname given to the biggest male singing and acting superstars in Hong Kong in the nineties. To them, I was a 24-year-old upstart who was trying to make changes in an industry I knew nothing about. "I have eaten more salt than you have eaten rice," they would retort in Mandarin, comparing their experience with my lack of it. I knew there was much I could learn from them. I doggedly hung around when they worked, observed what they did behind the scenes, lingered in the embalming room, and accompanied them when they transported the bodies. My mother never bothered with all that as she was content to sit in the office and deal with clients. But I have always felt it is important to understand the back of house, as well as the front of house, in order to run a business well.

It also helps that I have a strong stomach, perhaps due to the fact that the first dead body I had touched and seen was that of someone I loved—my father—which completely dispelled any fear I might have otherwise had of cadavers. This is a must for anyone working in the industry, whether they be male or female, although the general perception seems to be that women tend to have a lower tolerance for blood and gore.

But the first time I worked on an autopsied body, I was unfazed. I was in the Philippines on a business visit when the opportunity arose to participate in an embalming session. The deceased was a barrel-chested man in his forties who had died from injuries sustained during a bar fight. Post-mortems, also known as autopsies, are performed when someone has died under suspicious circumstances. During the post-mortem, which had been conducted by a pathologist, the body had been cut open at the abdomen with a large Y-shaped incision, and the organs had been removed, examined, and weighed before they were put back. To embalm the man, we had to reopen the stitches forming the Y-incision.

Before we started, one of the embalmers thrust a bottle of medicated oil at me. "Apply this under your nose, under your mask," she instructed. "It's going to smell bad." It did, but what I found more enlightening was seeing layers of rich yellow fat and other organs like the heart, lungs, and kidneys, which I had until then only read about in anatomy textbooks. As the deceased had drunk a lot of beer just before his death, his bladder was full, and we had to siphon out his urine with a drainage apparatus. The embalming process took four hours as he was a big man, and we had to ensure that every part of him was properly embalmed, right to the tips of his fingers. I remember he resembled Martin Luther King. What I was also quite amazed at was that the funeral home had a window through which the family could opt to witness the embalming. I remember his wife was watching initially, but she was too tired, perhaps drained, to observe afterwards.

I did not feel too comfortable with the idea of allowing family members to watch the embalming process. It reminded me of Breadtalk and Din Tai Fung's open concept kitchens, where people could watch bread being baked or dumplings being made behind glass windows. But those are food-related. This, on the other hand, involved surgical procedures. I understood the reason for this, though; there was a need to clear the air on what they were doing behind closed doors.

The Four Heavenly Kings used to call me "chilli padi," in reference to the tiny but extra spicy chilli, which is a metaphor for someone who is petite but feisty. The name stemmed from an episode when I saw one of the regular part-timers puffing on a cigarette in front of a client's family during a ceremony. I walked over to him and told the man, who was in his fifties, to stub it out. "If you want to smoke, please do it away from the sight of the family," I said. I felt that his smoking was disrespectful to the family.

I had no qualms about telling him how to do his job better, even though he was older than I was. My opinions were never based on the way things had been done before, but on the kind of service I would expect from a funeral director if I were a family member of the deceased.

I believed that Singapore's death care industry could be improved in many aspects. But my mother had a different idea. She did not want to see me organizing funerals for the rest of my life. She nagged, "There is no future in this line of work. It's a difficult industry, it's a sunset industry, and it's already saturated with too many competitors. I see you hanging around with old-timers and you always think you know better. You tell them what to do, which they don't like. You will lose your connection with society. You will never have any friends. You will never have a social life. And you will never find a husband."

She was relentless in getting me to quit the industry. I understood where she was coming from—she did not want me to do what she was doing, when the education and enrichment that she had given me earlier in my life provided me with other options. She also felt that it would be unwise for the same business to support so many people in the family. Sometimes I cried in the privacy of my room when I saw how stressed my mother was over my life choices. It was during those times that I missed my father the most.

I tried to placate her by doing what she wanted me to. In 2005, after one year of working in the funeral industry, I left her to join an independent financial advisory firm. She was happy, especially since I stayed at that job for four years. She thought I was contented and thriving, especially after my second year on the job when I made enough in commissions to qualify for the Million Dollar Round Table—an association of finance professionals who earn above certain levels in premiums, commissions, or income in a year—for the next three years.

But I couldn't stay away from the family trade. I continued hanging around the funeral parlor whenever I could, giving my mum endless suggestions on how to shake up the dated business model. In response, she would shake her head sorrowfully and tell me the same thing she had tried to drum into my head since I was a child: "You are too ambitious. You must have your feet planted firmly on the ground and not try to reach for instant success."

If there is one lesson I have learned from observing funerals, it is that we must live the life we want to live, because we only have one. I decided that I could make a bigger difference in the lives of people as a funeral director than as a financial advisor. In fact, with some experience in providing financial advice, I felt that I could provide a womb-to-tomb service in providing funeral and financial advisory services.

At the beginning of 2009, I turned my back on a steady five-figure monthly salary and decided to rejoin the funeral industry. Ma had nothing to say. I had already tried an alternative career, but both she and I knew my heart was not in it.

I wanted to do things differently from how they had been done over the last few decades, and I couldn't do that at my father's funeral company. I had to broaden my horizons. It was at this point that I formed a funeral consulting business overseas called TransLifeCare with my partners, who had decades of funerary and cemetery experience. I traveled to many countries, such as Malaysia, the Philippines, Vietnam, Australia, and New Zealand, to serve clients from different countries, observe how funerals are conducted overseas and attend funeral conferences.

After I sold my shares back to TransLifeCare, I plunged into funeral studies. I wanted to get certified as a funeral director because my mentor during my financial days once told me, "Do not wait for the government to regulate the industry. Be proactive and get the relevant certificates, even if the government is not regulating at that point in time."

So I went to Australia to take up a certification in Funeral Celebrant with Australian Celebrations Training, and took up a course at the Mount Royal University in Calgary, Canada, to become a certified funeral director. That was the year when my eyes were opened to the ideas I could bring back to Singapore.

All this had to be done overseas as, even now, there is no formal training required for funeral directors in Singapore. The industry is not regulated, and anyone can become a fly-by-night funeral director simply by doing the job of coordinating different service providers such as tentage and toilet providers, and embalmers. In the US, however, a person needs three years of education in a mortuary science school, followed by a year's internship, after which they sit for a state exam to become a licensed embalmer or funeral director.

It was also in 2009 that I changed my name. In Chinese tradition, names can be harbingers of fortune or doom. That's why celebrities sometimes change their names for better feng shui or luck. I was given the name Ang Mei Mei when I was born. It was apparently a bad name because "Mei Ang" sounds like "no husband" in Hokkien, which implies that I will never find a life partner. The number of strokes in the Chinese, combined with the time of my birth, were portents of ill fortune.

I had been told this twice before, and finally decided to take action when the third person, a Taoist master, also commented that my name was unlucky. I then officially changed my Chinese name from Hong Mei Mei to Hong Yu Xiu, which has a more auspicious number of strokes. I also decided to change the middle Mei of my name to Jolie, to reflect my admiration for actress Angelina Jolie's strength of character and her humanitarian work, and because "jolie" in French and "mei" in Chinese have the same meaning: beautiful. Thus, I reserved the name that my father gave me. From then on, I became Angjolie Mei.

In October 2010, I started my own company. I called it The Life Celebrant, because I believe that every life story deserves to be remembered. Its Chinese name, 心篇章 (*xīn piān zhāng*), means that the chapters of our lives should be cherished in our hearts. I had seen how funerals could be less about the mourning of a death, and more about the celebration of a life well lived. I was also determined that in order to do this, I had to offer unique services and stand out among those in the industry.

I started with my employees. I did not want to be a one-woman show, outsourcing to caterers, mobile toilet providers, and embalmers to run a funeral. I wanted to operate a sustainable business that could ultimately run without me, powered by experienced and competent staff who could come up with innovative ideas on their own.

I knew I would need at least six people to run what I thought would be an ideal funeral, including service staff who would do overnight shifts, greet visitors at the door, serve drinks and snacks, and even shelter visitors with umbrellas if necessary. I noticed that as the sizes of families shrank, they no longer had the manpower to attend to the needs of their guests. I also wanted to train funeral directors who could customize and personalize funerals. Every funeral should be unique, a representation of a life lived. It should not be a cookie-cutter funeral, indistinguishable from another.

In the beginning, I could only afford to hire part-timers and freelancers. At one large funeral, I managed to rope in two of my personal friends—one was between jobs and the other was an expatriate's wife—to help me serve drinks to visitors.

It was also an uphill task trying to hire funeral workers to join my start-up. There simply weren't that many people who were interested in working in this industry, unlike now, when we are seeing a spike in job applicants. More and more people are interested in pursuing this career. In the past, many funeral workers were not Singaporeans—they may have come from Malaysia or the Philippines—and many were from the older generation. Ex-prisoners were also drawn to the industry. Many people also had misconceptions, like someone whom I once interviewed, who formerly worked with a Christian funeral services provider. He told me, "I'm a Christian, so I cannot do Buddhist funerals nor hold joss sticks." I replied, "You will just be doing your job. I'm not asking you to change your faith." He eventually joined my company, and I am pleased to say he is now an expert on the intricacies of Buddhist funeral rites, such as who should bow, and when, and the offering of incense.

Whomever I do employ, I make sure they benefit from training. I used to train them myself, but nowadays I train the trainers. It's not enough for me that a person should lift caskets and do only that job for his entire working life. Between funerals, funeral workers usually have nothing to do and can wait around for hours, smoking cigarettes and shooting the breeze. I filled our office with a small library of books, both local and foreign, on funeral practices, and about life and death, as well as videos that I encouraged them to watch during their free time. Whenever I came across new material, I would pass it to them. As the industry is an evolving one, my employees need to keep their skills and knowledge up to date. At work, they were to put their best faces forward—no public displays of anger and frustration. Smoking was to be done discreetly.

Our practice is for the staff to stand in a row and bow to express appreciation and respect to the guests who are leaving. Once, when my team failed to bow when a busload of guests left the crematorium, I made sure to instruct them never to let it happen again.

I banned them from using dialect terms, which I feel degrade the service standards: to say "Singapore General Hospital" or "SGH" instead of *si pai por*, a colloquial Hokkien reference to the hospital which was derived from "Sepoy Plain," as a military camp called Sepoy Camp used to be located there. To say "transfer the body from the hospital" instead of *bua por*, which means to take the body from *si pai por* in Hokkien. To refer to the deceased, in relation to the family members, as "your mum" or "your dad," instead of "the corpse," or worse, *xi lang* ("dead person" in Hokkien). I also purchased new suits and jackets for my staff with touches of our corporate color, pink, so that they would appear more professional.

The team that has stayed with me has since developed into a tight-knit group, each with their own specialties: the one who knows all about Chinese funeral traditions; the one whose pleasant demeanor makes him the perfect client liaison; the one who was initially terrified of embalming, but who has since become competent at her job. Of late, my company has also attracted more women and young Singaporeans with degrees and diplomas who want to get a taste of the funeral services industry—like a former flight attendant who decided that her life's mission was to serve people with passion and purpose, and even interns from Hwa Chong Institution and Innova Junior College who were interested in learning more about the industry.

We reached a milestone when I conducted a funeral for the mother of a man who was a towering figure in the business community. I had butterflies in my stomach throughout the duration of the wake, but I had to prove to myself, and to my naysayers, that I could successfully organize such a large and high-profile event. Numerous VIPs, including politicians and business leaders, streamed in for the wake. My staff worked 12-hour shifts, and there were numerous requests from different family members that had to be met, including a last-minute request for a tribute video to be shown during the funeral two days later. We spent much time interviewing, filming family members, and editing the video—done at the funeral parlor itself to beat the deadline—to the family's satisfaction. The scariest part for me was when I stood in front of hundreds to deliver the final eulogy. By the time the funeral was over, we were all exhausted, but it was an achievement for our boutique company.

I also make it a point to tell as many people as possible about what funeral directors do, with an eye on raising awareness about the funeral industry through conversations about death. I frequently give talks at hospices and hospitals to the nurses and staff, so they have a better idea of how they can help their patients plan for their own funerals and give accurate information on what will happen after they die, funeral-wise. During career or entrepreneurship seminars, I share my journey with the students, tell them how I overcame obstacles and continued to fight on. I also chat with them so that they may be inspired by what I do, or simply go back home to think about their lives and whether they have shown enough love to their parents for it could be the last time they can do so.

To some, associating with people from the funeral industry is still *pantang*. When my mother decided to renovate the Ang Yew Seng funeral parlor in 2010, most of the interior designers we contacted were unwilling to take on the job. Only one finally decided to issue a price quote for the job, and even that was sky-high.

That is why my company name does not have the word "funeral" in it. When I used my father's business card in the past, which contained the word "funeral," some people returned my name cards to me because they felt the cards were bad luck.

Despite all the obstacles, there are more women running funeral services in Singapore than before, although the numbers are still small and people are still surprised when they discover what I do for a living. In the last 16 years, amongst all the people whom I have asked to guess my profession after I give out a few clues, only three have guessed correctly.

Many of these women, like me, are second generation funeral directors who are carrying on what their fathers did, and some are spouses of funeral directors. And perhaps because we stand out as women, we enjoy greater visibility. In Australia, there is even a company called White Lady Funerals that is helmed by female funeral directors. Their uniqueness lies in how, in their words, the "caring and compassionate" female funeral directors adopt a "softer, more specialized approach," which provides care for families in a "supportive and nurturing manner."

While I want to continue caring for each of my clients, I also feel the need to continue growing the business to provide better services to the increasingly discerning. I want to adopt innovative practices from overseas that may strike a chord with families here. I want to offer training courses in funeral studies so that my workers and those in the industry can become more competent in what they do. For instance, in Australia and New Zealand, embalmers need to go through theory classes and internships before they can practice. There is no requirement in Singapore at the moment. As such, I started an embalming class in 2019, and it was very well received. I am looking to ultimately start an academy for courses related to the provision of funeral services.

It is a bonus when I am recognized for what I do. In 2015, I was awarded a scholarship at a Professional Women's Conference in Chicago, acknowledging only female funeral directors. In July 2019, I was one of the winners for a local Women's Entrepreneur Award as well as a separate Most Innovative Award, for the changes I have introduced to the funeral industry. I was also one of the award recipients for the Spirit of Enterprise award. It was a real honor when I joined my fellow winners, incredibly capable and talented women across a diverse range of industries in Singapore, onstage.

I was once asked if I was a rose among the thorns. I replied that even if I were, the rose is never complete without the thorns. That is why women and men need to work together in the funeral industry. It's not about gender, but about whether the person taking care of a deceased's final farewell is able to do so in a competent and heartfelt way that beautifully closes the curtain on their life.

CHAPTER 3

Death Newbie

Since both my parents worked in the funeral industry, most people assume that I grew up around dead people, and would not be troubled by death.

But in the earlier part of my life, I had no inkling of what death meant or how to respond to it, and when people whom I knew died, I was traumatized. Nobody had ever explained to me what death meant or how I could cope with it. My experience of death and funerals was confined to picking up the occasional late-night phone call from someone asking for Pa to attend to a death. It was as ordinary as if he were an air conditioning technician and his client was calling him to attend to a repair.

When my great-grandfather, great-grandmother, and paternal grandparents died, I was so young that I don't remember having felt much emotion. The first 10 years of my childhood were spent in a happy, uneventful cocoon of school and play, untouched by the deaths that my parents dealt with every day. So when someone close to me died, I was woefully unprepared, and I still bear the emotional scars.

My best friend died when I was 11. I can still recall exactly what he had been like, down to some of the conversations that we had had. It is only human, I suppose, to remember most clearly those who have left us far too early. Huang Han Jie was my classmate at Ai Tong Primary School. We were opposites in so many ways—I was short-sighted and wore black-framed spectacles, while he had perfect eyesight; my grades were nothing to shout about, while he was a straight-A student.

But what we had in common was a mutual respect for law and order. We were very obedient students and nobody was surprised when we were elected class monitors when we were in Primary 3—titles that we continued holding for the next two years. Clad in our dark blue and white uniforms, we went around the school together, looking out for disobedient kids.

Once, I caught a boy talking during the school assembly. Friends hissed, "Eh, that is the son of the discipline mistress! You cannot book him or you'll get into trouble!" I was petrified. Han Jie, the voice of my conscience, said quietly, "We must book him. The rules apply to everyone."

Then came Thursday, 21 November 1991. We had just about finished our year in Primary 5 and the next day was the last day of school. We were looking forward to letting our hair down at the annual end-of-year school celebrations, where we would enjoy performances from various school groups like the choir, dance group, and school band, before starting a six-week holiday break.

At home that evening, I couldn't wait to go to school for the celebrations the next day. I had my dinner and was watching the usual Mandarin television programs on Channel 8 when our house phone rang. The call was for me, which was unusual. I normally did not chat with my friends on the phone, only at school.

My friend on the other end of the line was frantic. "Mei Mei, Han Jie is dead!"

"You're crazy. Don't talk nonsense." I refused to believe him.

The boy, who had heard the news from another friend, yelled, "It's true! I heard that he died in a car accident!"

At that time, we did not have mobile phones, but the news spread quickly. Those in our class panicked and called one another, trying to ascertain if the rumor was true. We all called Han Jie's home, but no one picked up.

There was nothing else left to do but to agree to meet in school early the next day to wait for Han Jie. The plan was to give him hell for making us worry.

The next morning, even before the sky had lightened, eight of us turned up at school. Han Jie usually arrived early. In our desperation to see him walk into the school, we had all acquired a false sense of bravado.

"If what you said isn't true, I'm going to beat you up," I said, mock punching the boy who had called me the night before.

We waited anxiously, talking about Han Jie and how he would be starting the new year in 6A, the top class. We chatted nervously, relentlessly, about our last-day-of-school celebrations, about anything, so that time would pass more quickly. By 6:45 am, when Han Jie would normally have arrived at school, we had quieted down. By 7 am, we knew. When the school bell rang, signaling the start of the school day, and Han Jie had still not turned up, our tears started falling quietly.

The discipline master then announced during the school assembly that morning that Han Jie had died. The rest of our schoolmates, who had no idea why the group of us had been weeping earlier, mourned along with us.

We found out from the newspapers the next day what had happened: At about 6:30 pm, Han Jie had taken a public bus home, which he did every day after school. He was crossing the road at a pedestrian crossing when he was run over by a cement mixer lorry. The driver had not seen him. Han Jie's head had been crushed, his father told the newspaper reporter. The image of his distraught parents in the newspaper still stays on my mind.

Because Han Jie had died on the second-to-last day of term, the school did not hold any events to commemorate his death—no remembrance, farewell, or memorial. As we started our school holidays, we were left to cope with our personal grief.

I did not know what to do. I had no inkling of funeral niceties. My ma gave me some money in an envelope, the *pek-kim* (white gold), which is a customary gift of condolence money to the deceased's family at the wake, to give to Han Jie's family. I went to his flat with a group of friends but no one was home. I slipped the envelope under the door and left.

Death weighs heavily on a child's soul. Perhaps even more than adults do, children crave closure, understanding, and acceptance. They have difficulty understanding why someone they cared about is gone forever. They need an explanation as to what has happened.

I was not able to contact Han Jie's family. Because of the tragic manner in which he had died, his family had not held a funeral wake. We heard that he had been cremated immediately. I had no idea where his final resting place was.

I found solace in playing melancholy songs on the piano. I was so distraught that I lost my appetite and sometimes skipped meals. I missed Han Jie. My mother knew I was grieving, but she didn't know how to console her own daughter despite the fact that my parents were in the funeral business. Ours was a traditional Chinese family. We just didn't talk about death and our emotions easily.

No one mentioned Han Jie when school reopened the following year. It was as if talking about him would bring bad luck—as if the best thing to do was to pretend he had never existed and to move on with life.

I felt an uncontrollable anger at losing my friend, but I did not know how to express it. Occasionally, I would pick up rocks and fling them at cement mixer lorries, as if punishing the one that had killed him. All I could think was, "You took my friend away." I even bought him a birthday gift—a Garfield mug with the Aries star sign, as his birthday fell one day before my father's. I celebrated with him in the emptiness in my room, singing a birthday song to him. I had the mug placed on my desk for many years to come.

Years later, when my schoolmates and I met up as adults, we found out we had all mourned silently, expressing our grief in different ways. Our parents and teachers had not realized how traumatized we were, as children, by the death of our friend.

After Han Jie died, I unconsciously avoided forming close friendships and shunned my usual playmates. After school, I used to spend the afternoon at my grandmother's flat, which was on the second floor. Tabitha and Amanda were her neighbors, and they often shouted for me from the ground floor to join them at the playground. But after Han Jie died, I no longer played with or talked to them. Even today, while I socialize, I am always wary of getting close to too many people. I am afraid I will get hurt when someone I care for dies.

A few years later, when I was 15, my mother's second sister was diagnosed with ovarian cancer at the age of 39. The illness was discovered after she had experienced an episode of intense bleeding and had to be hospitalized. One of the defenses I put up in the wake of Han Jie's death was the denial that death would befall anyone in my family, but it unavoidably did. After her diagnosis, I withdrew further into my shell.

I was very close to my aunt. Like me, she was the second child in the family. No one imagined she would fall ill for she was very fit, frequently climbing mountains and running marathons. She ran a provision shop in Ang Mo Kio selling biscuits and coffee powder where I spent much time, and of which I had many happy memories. I would hang out at her shop at least once a week before my enrichment classes, and sometimes I helped to mind the shop. Even today, when I tie a packet of biscuits in a way that guarantees its freshness, I remember how it was she who had taught me that skill.

When she was ill for seven years, she did not give up. I saw how cancer took a healthy person over physically, but not mentally; when she was ill and very frail, she still enjoyed going on staycations with us. She refused to be confined to a wheelchair, so whenever she was feeling breathless, my sisters and I would take turns carrying her. She once asked me when I was a kid if I would take care of her when she grew old. I wish I had her tenacity and her determination. She was the pillar of our family.

I took the news of her illness very badly. I avoided my friends at school. I refused to tell anyone about this news because I knew nobody would understand what I was going through, just like how I dealt with the death of Han Jie. Nobody would empathize and help me with it. I started binge eating and put on 20 lbs in one month. My name means "beautiful" in Chinese, and when I put on weight, I was cruelly taunted for being the antithesis of that. "Mei Mei" was now "Chou Chou" ("Ugly Ugly"). In response to the weight gain and the bullying, I became bulimic. During recess at school, I preferred to study alone, or look for teachers to talk about schoolwork. I didn't want people to see me eating. I poured my energies into my studies. I would binge once I reached home, only to throw up afterwards.

My elder sister caught me putting a finger down my throat and purging into the toilet bowl a few times. She told our mother, who threatened to send me to a dietitian. I saw the dietitian twice but, in the end, pragmatism put an end to my bulimia as I refused to waste money on consulting one. I lived with the eating disorder for four years.

My aunt died in 2003, when I was 23.

The next death that shook my life was my father's. He died a year after my aunt did. I was not even done with grieving my aunt, and now I had to grieve for my father. That was when I finally accepted that death sometimes comes knocking uninvited, but life has to go on.

CHAPTER 4

Children and Death

*I*n October 2019, I gave birth to my first child. Becoming a parent is a life-changing experience, in every way, for everyone. But when it came to my job as a funeral director and celebrant, handling the funerals of babies and children became perilously personal. It is an unspoken fear amongst all of us in the funeral industry—one that is mostly unvoiced because it is so deeply personal and, perhaps, unlucky to speak of. Every child's funeral we handle inevitably forces the question: What if it were our own child?

This came to the fore most forcefully when I was called to conduct the funeral of a four-month-old girl who had died of sudden infant death syndrome (SIDS), which is the unexplained death of children below one, usually when they are asleep. This child had died in her sleep in March 2020.

Her parents, who were Christians and believed that their baby had gone to a better place, chose to celebrate and commemorate her life. She was lovingly bathed and dressed by our staff, after which her parents came in to hold and hug her. I was not physically present in the room, but I was watching the scene unfold from the CCTV in my office. The baby girl was just a few weeks younger than my own beloved girl. I was so emotionally wrought by what I saw that I went straight home to hug my daughter tightly that night.

The little girl's wake, which lasted two days and one night at our Showers of Love sanctuary, was well attended by over 50 people. When I finally had a chance to speak to the baby girl's mother, I told her, "I'm sorry for your loss. I really feel your pain as a mother—I'm a new mum with a four-month-old child." At this point, no words were needed as we, teary-eyed, hugged each other. She did not cry during the wake, but when she hugged me, she said, "I really want to cry, but I need to be strong." She had two older girls who were not at the funeral of their baby sister.

While being a mother gives baby and child funerals greater personal resonance, it is always trying to handle the funerals of the young ones. The first time I saw a dead baby, 15 years before I had one of my own, I was overwhelmed with sorrow.

The baby's father, who asked us to arrange for the funeral of his firstborn son, looked about my age. I was 24 then. The baby had been born premature and his frail body, even with the help of the hospital's machines, was unable to sustain his life. His mother lay in hospital, still recuperating from delivering the baby and the emotional trauma of losing him, and was unable to attend the funeral. The waxy yellow body of the baby, clad in white and blue, was small enough to fit snugly in my hand. The child resembled a doll with its perfectly formed fingers and toes. As he lay in the small, white coffin, the thought crossed my mind that the hard box was a most uncomfortable final resting place for a baby.

When I later attended a funeral directors' conference in the US, I came across an American company that sold padded caskets customized for babies—cushioned affairs in pink or blue fabric that resemble bassinets rather than hard boxes—and I decided to bring them to Singapore. It is a difficult thing to bury one's child, and these child-friendly caskets help to soften the edge off such funerals.

Singapore has one of the lowest infant mortality rates in the world, but that does not make the death of a child any less tragic. Dwight D. Eisenhower once said, "There is no tragedy in life like the death of a child." Nature and God intended that children grow up and outlive their parents. There is even a Chinese proverb, 白发人送黑发人 (the white-haired sending off the black-haired), which eloquently depicts the sadness of the situation in which children die before their parents.

No one expects to have to plan a funeral for their child, and those who have to usually do so in a state of shock, being overwrought and in denial.

The funeral of a baby or a child in a traditional Chinese family would be quite different from that of an adult's, as elders cannot show their respect to those who are younger. While the death of an elderly person is accompanied by loud wailing, prayers, and all of the associated rituals, the burial or cremation of a baby or a young child is to be conducted in silence without any funeral rites, and parents are advised to leave the venue before the start of the funeral. The deceased child should be buried or cremated swiftly, without the traditional wake, and the funeral might only last several hours.

Likewise, when a young unmarried person dies, their parents should not offer prayers, and the body will be placed at the funeral parlor for the wake, as it cannot be brought home. A husband or wife should not pay respects to their spouse either, as they are considered equals.

However, these practices have evolved over time. Embalming a child, if done, is often more challenging for the embalmer than embalming an adult. Psychologically, it is painful to work on the body of a dead child, especially if the embalmer is a parent. Technically, a child's blood vessels are smaller and are harder to locate for the embalming procedure.

If the deceased was a newborn, once the body has been cleaned and readied, I always ask the father if he wants to take a photograph of his child, as the mother may still be in hospital and unable to catch the last glimpse of her baby. Some families are too distraught to think of documenting the funeral, while others may consider it improper to photograph a dead body. But it helps those who are grieving to achieve emotional closure if they are able to see their loved one—child or adult—for the last time, before they are buried or cremated. When Han Jie died, there was no wake or funeral at which I could say goodbye to him, and my grief was not acknowledged or addressed.

At times, I also suggest to the parents that the funeral be conducted after the mother is discharged from the hospital, so mummy gets to say goodbye too.

The emotional challenges that the family members of a dead child have to face can be daunting. The grief that sets in when a child dies always cuts more deeply than that of an adult who has lived a good number of years. For the mother, who may have felt the baby growing in her belly and started calling her child by name, and for the other members of the family who may have already begun imagining a life with the newest member of the family, the death of the baby is also the loss of hope in the future. A miscarriage, which may occur at a very early stage of pregnancy, can be just as emotionally devastating.

A client gave me a glimpse into the emotional hell he was going through. "I need to organize a funeral for my daughter," he said when he called me. "She is one of a pair of newborn twins. Her sister survived, but she did not." The deceased was born full-term, but her brain had not fully developed, and she died shortly after her birth.

I met him at the café of a hospital to discuss the funeral. He could not go to my office as he had to stay at the hospital with his wife and surviving child. He confided tearfully, "Can you imagine what I'm going through? I have to organize a funeral for one daughter while welcoming the other into this world."

As a funeral director, I felt there was more I could do for the families of children who have died. In 2017, I started a special children-centered funeral service which I called Angel Star or 天使心. The name means that the children who have departed are like angels or stars in heaven. They will forever be looking down upon us. It fittingly links with the name of a Singapore organization that has done great work in caring for children with terminal illnesses and their families, called Star Pals.

Angel Star helps parents commemorate the life of their children, no matter how brief it is. What parents really appreciate is how they can get involved in bathing and dressing their children at our special Showers of Love sanctuary. Even though they have not lived many years, a child's life is worth celebrating because every life, no matter how brief, has meaningful stories.

One of the Angel Star funerals I conducted was for a boy named Neal Chia, who died of bone cancer in February 2017. He was only 11 years old, but there was so much of his life to celebrate.

When I went to the family home to discuss the funeral arrangements, I saw heaps of golf trophies and golf clubs, which I initially thought belonged to Neal's father but which in fact were Neal's. It wasn't only golf; he was also an avid basketball player and budding guitarist.

During the funeral, we also put up a display of his Rubik's cubes—he had picked it up after he contracted bone cancer and could no longer pursue his favorite sports. And everyone who came to say goodbye left with a Rubik's cube, instead of the traditional red string given out at Chinese funerals.

Angel Star also addressed a gap in the market for women whose babies died in the womb, are stillborn, or are unwanted pregnancies. For fetuses that might have died in utero—perhaps their little hearts stopped beating, they suffered umbilical cord accidents, or mummy had a miscarriage—the standard procedure is for the bodies to be treated as biohazardous waste and be disposed of, or the remains might be kept in a small clinical container. Few parents and even gynecologists know that they can organize a cremation for these fetuses, and have a proper farewell for them.

I realize that even for unborn children, parents and family members long for proper closure—a proper event where they can express their love and wishes for their baby before the baby is cremated. And it is critical that the mother is there too.

The usual process is that the fetus is transferred to our care before a funeral date is confirmed. We use dry ice to keep the fetus' body cool and to retard decomposition. In most cases, the funeral is held the next day, and the cremation could be on the same day, or the day after.

This service has been increasingly popular since it was introduced, with up to six fetus funerals per month. For these parents, it is clear that even if their babies did not live to see a single day, the funerals that celebrate their lives give their existence a sense of significance.

This all relates to when a child dies. But what about when someone in the family dies, and the children struggle to cope? The adults don't always know how to respond.[5]

The biggest mistake adults can make is to try to protect children by not explaining what death means, or by using euphemisms. For example, children might be told, "Grandpa is going away for a long time" or "Grandpa is sleeping." But when they witness the cremation or burial, they may become terrified that the same might happen to them when they are asleep.

---

5 There are numerous support groups for parents who have lost their child, including Child Bereavement Center, a group started by grieving parents. Their website is www.childbereavement.org.

The Chinese traditionally believe that spirits lurk around funeral wakes, and children are greatly discouraged from going to one lest they be possessed by malevolent forces. But children need an honest explanation as to what is going on, and they need to be able to say farewell to the person who has died.

I was determined that the same would not happen to my brother, Zachary, who is 15 years younger than I am. He grew up at our family's funeral parlor at Sin Ming Drive—he went there after school every day as my mother was then already helping my father in the office, and as he did his homework, bodies would be brought in and out from the parlor. But he was clueless about death until our father died when he was nine years old.

I knew he didn't fully understand what had happened. Because I had always been an authority figure in his life, given our age gap, I tried to guide him through our father's death. On one of the paper plates at the funeral—the sort typically used to hold melon seeds at a funeral wake—I drew a simple life cycle. Because my father was Buddhist, I based it on the Buddhist idea of reincarnation.

"You see, Zachary, first we are born. We go to school like you are doing now, then after school you will start work, just like me. Along the way, you might meet someone special and get married, like how Ma and Pa met and married each other. One day, you will grow old and when you get very sick like Pa, you will die. Then you will be born again as a baby and the whole cycle starts again."

He asked innocently, as he pointed to the figure of the reborn baby I had drawn, "Which baby is Papa now?" I replied, "We don't know, but I hope that one day, we will be together."

He still didn't understand. Full realization only hit him on the last day of the seven-day wake, during the funeral, before the cremation. Zachary desperately wanted to eat fried chicken, but he couldn't as we were only eating vegetarian food during the mourning period, which is a Buddhist practice for family members of the deceased. This was to give Pa good karma in his next life.

When we turned down Zachary's request for fried chicken, he started to cry—slowly at first, then he started sobbing so hard he couldn't speak. He started to hiccup and was inconsolable. I knew then that there was something else bothering him. I lifted him up, carried him to a quiet corner and asked, "What's the matter?"

He cried out, "I have no Papa!"

It broke my heart to hear him say this. While I held him tighter and reassured him that there were many other people who loved him, I was also relieved at his outburst because it meant he had understood.

I once conducted the funeral for a baby who had died while choking on milk. Wrestling with guilt and grief, her parents decided that they would not let their four-year-old daughter see her brother in the casket. But I could hear the girl, who was being looked after by their domestic helper, crying outside the funeral parlor.

I explained to her parents, "Your daughter needs to say goodbye to her brother. I can help."

As the little girl was led up to her brother's blue casket, she gazed at his lifeless body. "What happened to Didi?" she asked. Both parents started to tear, too overcome with grief to answer. I gave the girl a piece of paper and told her, "Do you want to say something to Didi? What did you love about him? You can draw or write what you feel about Didi."

I left the family to mourn in private. While I believe that children should be told what is happening, I refrain from giving explanations if these may be at odds with the family's religious or personal beliefs. The paper with the girl's scribbling was later placed in the casket before her brother was cremated. The girl had quieted down and did not say anything, but her questions, and eventual realization that her brother had died, would come later.

From my experience, these are some ways to help a child cope with death:

Talk to the child honestly

Help the child understand what is happening. Answer their questions. How you choose to do so may depend on your religious affiliation, or you could also explain death from a scientific perspective. The child has to be gently led to accept that death is permanent.

Cry with the child

There is no need to cry in secret. Allowing the child to see you cry encourages them to express their own feelings.

Be gentle

As an adult, you may be struggling to cope with funeral and post-death arrangements, but always be patient with children. Try to refrain from angry outbursts, as you may regret them. They may not yet be able to fully verbalize what they are feeling, in which case you could encourage dialogue by saying, "I am feeling sad because Grandpa is dead. How are you feeling?" Alternatively, you could ask them to express themselves by drawing.

Bring the child to the wake to bid farewell

Unless you have traditional beliefs, I feel that it is appropriate to bring children to the wake, no matter how young they might be, especially if they knew the deceased well. The wake is an occasion for all to bid farewell to the deceased, even though some people may think that the presence of a child may be rude and disruptive to a wake's solemn proceedings, and superstitious older folk might think it is unlucky for the child to be there.

At funeral parlors in Japan, there are often corners or rooms with toys and games to keep the child occupied while their parents pay their respects to the deceased and comfort the family, and it inspired me to include something similar at the wakes I organize.

Let the child participate in the wake and funeral

Give the child an avenue to express their fondest memories of the deceased, for example by writing or drawing, and folding the papers into origami, or sticking notes or messages onto the casket. Children's memories can be very touching and surprisingly insightful.

Once, at the funeral of an elderly man, one of his grandsons, who was about seven years old, wrote a note: "I love Gong Gong because he taught me how to play mahjong." The child's guileless contribution added another humorous memory to the family's repository about Gong Gong, which even his own children might not have known about. It also gave the child a chance to say farewell in his own way.

Remain vigilant

After the funeral, keep a close eye on the child. If they show any change in behavior—not being able to sleep or eat, or being withdrawn—you may need to seek professional help. Helping the child to understand death and cope with grief will go a long way in guiding them to cope with the losses that will inevitably come along in their life.

CHAPTER 5

Preserving the Dead

I n January 2019, a young and up-and-coming Singapore actor who was on military duty in New Zealand died from training injuries. Two days after he died, his body was sent back to Singapore. His body had already been embalmed and dressed in New Zealand. This is the regulation—anyone who dies in another country must be embalmed and sealed in the casket before the casket is allowed on the plane. The Sealing Certificate and Embalming Certificate must be presented before a permit is issued.

But as someone in the industry with some knowledge of standards and practices, I offered the funeral director, who was handling his funeral, to help touch up and care for him. For me, it is essential to prepare someone on their final journey with care and love. Even when a body has been embalmed and repatriated to Singapore, our standard practice is to open the casket and check and assess the condition of the body, because the process of transportation can be disruptive: Is there a need to touch up the makeup? Tweak the hairstyle? Arrange the clothing?

Like the rest of the nation, I also felt deeply for this young man and the circumstances that had led to his death. This was an area of expertise in which I could help.

Once his casket was brought to our facility, we opened it and the bag in which his body had been placed. Yes, he had been embalmed. But we saw that there was much we could do to make him look better. He had been dressed in an incongruous purple shirt and a white suit. We changed his clothing so he would be wearing his favorite black shirt and black pants, which had been passed to us by his manager who was standing beside us throughout.

His hair was not styled in a way which he would normally have worn it, and I would not begrudge that as there was no way the embalmer in New Zealand would have had any knowledge of this. The actor's usual hairstylist was asked to come to our facility where, once she got over her tears, she styled his hair exactly the way he usually wore it. As he had some stubble, we also shaved him properly, and airbrushed spots on his skin which had not been properly made-up.

Few saw the work we put in, as his casket was closed to the thousands of people who turned up at his wake to say goodbye. But it did not matter, as long as we knew in our hearts that we had done our best.

Preparing a body for its final journey, or embalming, is both a science and an art. It is the science of preserving human remains to delay the process of decomposition, and it is an art to make the deceased presentable for viewing.

People are embalmed for many reasons—sometimes for medical or scientific study, sometimes for religious purposes. But when it comes to funerals, a body is embalmed for three key reasons: sanitization, preservation, and presentation. This is so that it can last throughout the wake and is safe for family members to touch. It also gives people peace of mind when they see their loved ones in tranquil repose.

There are people who choose not to embalm their loved ones because they have certain misconceptions about the process, chief of which is that embalmers remove organs. I know of funeral directors who are asked by only half, or even fewer, of their clients to embalm the bodies in their care. I strongly recommend embalming, and my company embalms nearly all of the bodies that come under our care, because the process is explained clearly to the family members so that they understand why it is done. I strongly believe that everyone deserves a proper and dignified final bath.

I respectfully remind clients that as their loved ones are no longer alive, the body's processes are no longer functioning nor the muscles working. That means that while they are in the casket, bodily fluids may leak and the body might start to smell. Singapore has a hot and humid climate, and most funeral wakes are held at the void decks of public flats that are not air-conditioned. If the family of the deceased still chooses not to have their loved one embalmed, their wishes will, of course, be adhered to. In those instances, the casket is hermetically sealed, and I advise the family to keep the wake preferably to a maximum of three days.

When a person dies, they stop breathing, and the oxygen levels in their body decrease. As neurons in the brain lose function, hormones are no longer released into their body. A chemical that is necessary for the relaxation of muscle fibers after a contraction, adenosine triphosphate (ATP), is depleted. As a result, every single muscle in the body relaxes, including the sphincters. Urine and fecal matter may leak.

Because the heart has stopped pumping, livor mortis occurs, which is when the blood settles at the lowest point of the body, leaving a deep reddish-purple mark called a post-mortem stain. A person who was on their back after they died would have post-mortem stains on the back or on the backs of the legs.

After three to six hours, the limbs stiffen as calcium leaks into the muscle cells and binds with protein in a state called rigor mortis. This sets into the face two to four hours after death, and hits the bigger muscle groups in about six to 12 hours.

The skin also dries out, shrinking and pulling away from the hair and nails, so it may look as if the hair and nails of the deceased have grown.

At this point, if the body is left alone—for example, if the person's death has gone undiscovered—the cells begin to die and the body starts to decay. Around 100 trillion external microbes start eating away at it. The bacteria in the gut begin to digest the intestines and abdominal organs, and this is when the smell of rotting flesh starts to emanate from the body.

The breakdown of amino acids then attracts insects like mites and blowflies, which begin laying eggs in the rotting flesh. In a few weeks, the maggots can eat around 60 percent of the body. After 20 to 50 days, dry decay begins, attracting beetles and fungi. In a few years, plants and animals will feed off the remains, including the bones.

Embalming slows this process. We do our embalming in what I call a Care Center—we are, after all, caring for someone—which is the embalming room of my father's funeral parlor at Sin Ming Drive. The road is also popularly known by locals as Death Alley, as the area is home to a multitude of funeral offices and parlors, shared embalming rooms, companies that make joss paper items[6] for burning, and a florist. When the body is transferred from the hospital or where the death has occurred, it will be carried out of the van (usually by two men)

---

6 Traditionally, these are imitation money notes that are burned for the dead, but they can also come in the form of paper reproductions of everyday items, like clothing, accessories, or electronics.

on a stretcher down a corridor, past a wooden sliding door, into the Center.

The Sin Ming Drive area is also home to many car repair workshops and a vehicle inspection center. Those patrons eating at the coffee shop while waiting for their cars to be serviced won't realize anything amiss, because the deceased's body will be covered from head to toe. White cloth is wrapped around the deceased if they died a natural death, while a white zipped body bag is used if the body is highly decomposed.

The Center is about the size of a bedroom. It is cold and sterile, like a hospital operating theater, and the sliding door is always shut to protect the privacy of the deceased. The stark white fluorescent lights illuminate two steel embalming tables on rollers, on which we place the bodies. These tables have an inch-high border so that water, blood, and fluids don't flow onto the floor but into a drainage point at the foot of the embalming table, into a pail. This liquid is then thrown into a bin specially meant for biohazardous waste, which will later be incinerated.

In one corner of the room is the all-important embalming machine, which resembles a stainless steel box. Shelves and cupboards line two of the room's four walls. These are filled with tubs and plastic boxes in which we store embalming chemicals and tools. In a corner are the materials we use to beautify the body, such as special makeup for the dead, lots of plastic combs and brushes, a hair dryer, and hair styling mousse.

A plethora of shiny steel surgical instruments, from forceps to hooks to S-shaped needles to 16-inch needles, are laid out as part of our embalming kit. Many of these instruments are specialized: for instance, after preserving the organs of an autopsied body and placing them back into the body cavity, we use an S-shaped needle to suture the surfaces of the skin together, because skin, unlike cloth, cannot be gathered and bent.

We are only as good as our tools, which is why I insist that our embalmers use good equipment, and I import tools and chemicals if necessary.

Bottles of fluids, in colors ranging from blue to orange to pink, sit on our shelves. Each has a special property. There is a pinkish cream that is used on the eyes, lips, and nostrils to smooth unsightly wrinkles and folds. There are arterial-tinted chemicals that replace the blood in the body and impart a "glow" to grey and sallow skin. We also have a special, ultrapotent arterial embalming fluid that works better than the normal kind on refrigerated and frozen bodies, as well as on putrefied tissue. Another type of embalming fluid was developed to reduce swollen tissues because embalmers were seeing an increase in the number of bodies swollen from oedema, due to new medications and hospital techniques.

Many have asked me whether I have seen ghosts in the Care Center and in the course of my work. I have never felt any supernatural presence that has raised the hairs on the back of my neck or caused gooseflesh on my arm, although some with a more powerful antenna for the ghostly claim that they have sensed dead people in the Center.

An embalmer can work alone, but a petite embalmer would benefit from working with an assistant, as she would need to lift and turn the body when putting on the clothes. The top occupational hazard for one working in the funeral industry is back injury, usually sustained from having to frequently lift heavy bodies. In some other countries, lifting devices—where straps are placed under bodies weighing more than 220 lbs and hoisted by a machine—are commonplace, but these are not frequently used in Singapore, where bodies weigh an average of 130 to 155 lbs.

I decided to get a lifting device when I started Showers of Love—a new service where family members can be involved in the preparation of their loved one's body for the final farewell, with guidance from our staff. Because the staff in Showers of Love are mainly ladies, I was concerned with the handling of heavy bodies. Since we got the device, it has helped my team to be more efficient with their work.

Before the embalmers enter the Care Center, we put on hospital scrubs before donning another layer of protective gear: blue long-sleeved, tissue-like garments, surgical face masks, gloves that come up to the middle of the forearm, and boots. This is to protect ourselves from germs, blood, and bodily fluids. We are professionals who love our jobs, but we also take its risks very seriously. My sister, who is an embalmer, has even invested in a full-face mask, with a respirator for breathing, to fully protect herself from chemical fumes and gases. My company's embalmer has also invested in a full-face mask.

In the past, people operated according to what they were comfortable with, or how they had been taught. If they were at ease with smoking while doing embalming work in their slippers and shorts, they did. In fact, embalming used to be carried out at HDB void decks, under a canvas structure, or in homes. It was also a cost-saving measure for funeral directors, because such locations did not incur rental costs, unlike proper embalming rooms. Under these conditions, the bodies frequently could not be showered, and were only wiped down. Blood and other waste products were poured directly into the drains.

After we don our gear, we start work, which can take place at any hour. Some embalmers try to complete the job in as short a time as possible—in as little as 30 minutes—because the funeral directors they work for are under the misconception that the family members want their loved ones back home as quickly as possible. But I believe that embalming is a complex process and the embalmers need sufficient time—at least one and a half to two hours—to do a good job. Once I explain the tedious process of embalming to the family members, they understand and even ask us to take our time to embalm their loved ones. They are usually agreeable to wait a little longer. In cases where a post-mortem is conducted and if reconstruction is required, the time taken is even longer.

First, we unwrap the body and cut the white twine that has been used to tie together the big toes on each foot so that the legs don't splay during transport. Sometimes, the wrists are tied together, and this poses a huge problem for embalmers as the cloth used to bind the wrists will leave dent marks. We also remove the diaper that was put on by the hospital staff to absorb body fluids and feces. When we put the body on the embalming table, we prop up the head on a head block, which is slightly larger than a brick but is light and strong, so the blood will not collect there and stain the face. The embalming table is tilted so that the fluids can drain easily. The face and the hands must be stain-free as these can be seen when the casket is opened. We even scrub the nails to ensure that the hands look clean.

A disinfectant is first sprayed onto the body to make sure it is safe for handling, followed by a moisturizing liquid for the dry skin. Then we give the deceased a bath. Those who have been hospitalized or incapacitated with terminal illnesses might not have enjoyed a good bath for months. On the wall next to each bed in the Care Center is a showerhead, similar to the kind in your bathroom, so we can shampoo and condition the hair, soap and rinse the body. Then we towel dry the body and hair.

After the shower, we need to set the features by closing the eyes and mouth. This has to be done before the infusion of the embalming chemicals that will firm up the flesh. If cheeks are hollow, wads of cotton wool go into the mouth to plump them up.

We have to replace most of the blood in the body with embalming chemicals, which is a mixture of formaldehyde, other preservative chemicals, and water. About two gallons of embalming chemicals are required. First, we have to find a big "pipe" in the body, which is the carotid artery. Guided by experience, we have to feel for the artery, which is about 0.5 cm thick, near the collarbone. We make an incision in the skin, pull out the artery and make a small cut in it. Blood will not course out of dead bodies because the heart is no longer beating. The cut creates a break in the continuous loop of the artery, which allows us to pump in the embalming chemicals. Later, this incision will be sutured, and the suture mark covered up by clothing.

Then, we insert one end of the tube from the embalming machine into the artery. The machine starts to pump in embalming chemicals. As the chemicals enter the body, blood and excess arterial solution are displaced from the right jugular vein, which we would also have located and made a cut in for the outflow. Our embalming machine is a top-of-the-line piece of technology that allows us to choose from low or high pressure, or pulsation (like a heartbeat) versus continuous flow. As the chemicals enter the body, we massage the flesh to aid the circulation of the chemicals into the body tissues.

The pace at which an embalmer works is important. An embalmer who rushes may end up rupturing blood vessels because of the high-pressure jet. Most people don't have perfectly clear circulatory systems because arteries and vessels are sometimes clogged with cholesterol, or tumors get in the way, which may slow down the embalming process. When the color of the emergent fluid changes from red to a lighter color, we know that the blood in the entire system has been replaced. We can further confirm this by scrutinizing the color of the skin, to see if it has taken on the pinkish tinge imparted by the colored embalming chemicals, and gently pressing on the flesh. If we touch a tender spot, which isn't firm like the other embalmed areas, we know we might have to employ a hypodermic needle to inject the embalming chemicals directly to that area. Nails that appeared bluish would turn pink too, proof that the chemicals have reached the fingertips.

We also have to be very judicious in our choice of chemicals, which depends on the condition of the body. For example, if the body is bloated, there are specific chemicals that we can use to reduce the swelling. If the person died of liver illness, there will be a yellowish tinge to the skin, so we will have to use different chemicals or the skin will turn greenish.

Once the carotid artery is closed and the skin sutured shut, we move on to the intestinal area. This is where embalming is most crucial because the intestines are packed with colonies of bacteria that don't die when the person does. Without embalming, bacteria continue to thrive, the body bloats with gases, and serious rot and discoloration of the body—from green to black—can set in quickly.

To embalm the abdominal cavity, we use a hollow needle called a trocar that is about 16 inches long. We insert it near the navel to remove gas, fluids, and semi-solids, and then we introduce the embalming chemicals. Once we have finished, we seal the wound with a button shaped like a small pagoda, with ridges to catch securely onto the edges of the flesh. We then bathe the body one last time to wash off residual blood and embalming chemicals.

We dress the deceased in clothes that the family members have provided. This is done before the application of cosmetics, as we do not want to smear the makeup. There is an order in which clothes are put on. For instance, belts are pre-looped through the pants so that we can avoid having to lift the body twice. We also put the deceased's undergarments on them. It is an item that many people forget because they think it is not required, but we include it out of respect and the dignity of the deceased.

We have also had to make alterations for those who may have "outgrown" their clothes. A deceased gentleman, who was rather portly and had a significant beer belly, had a wife who insisted that he be buried in his army uniform from over 30 years ago. It was clear from the uniform that he had been significantly leaner then. I explained to her that the shirt would not fit, and that she would have to give me a new set of clothing or we would have to cut the back of the uniform open. She chose the second option. After making the cut and dressing the deceased with the uniform, we tacked the slit so the shirt would not slip and it would not be apparent that it had been altered.

Once the body has been dressed, we "color" the pale face with cosmetic products. In the past, when embalming chemicals with a higher concentration of formaldehyde were used, we would have had to use thicker makeup to compensate for the darkening of the skin. With less formaldehyde in today's chemicals, which are also tinted to impart a tinge of pink to the skin, makeup can be applied with a lighter touch.

The easiest and fastest way to style the hair of the deceased is to comb all their hair back, but it is not the best way. When I started in the industry, I was curious why every departed person had the same "backcomb" hairstyle. I then realized that the embalmer was not given a photograph as a reference, and that the embalmer feels that his job is only to sanitize and preserve, and not to present the deceased. I beg to differ, which is why I insist on making sure we follow the hairstyle of the departed. Otherwise, the dead may end up with a hairstyle like that of a vampire, especially if they have a widow's peak. If the hair is voluminous, it might stand up unattractively. This can be a bit of a shock when family members gaze upon the face of their dad who always used to have a fringe, or their mum who always kept her hair neatly in a bun.

We do our work while referring to a photo of the deceased, provided by the family, as it is important that the result resembles the hairstyle in the photo. We even have hairspray to darken the hair, which we often use upon request from family members for those deceased who used to take a lot of pride in their appearance. That is also why we invite family members to our Showers of Love sanctuary, where they can participate in the presentation of their departed loved one. Ensuring that their loved one wears the hairstyle and makeup that is familiar to everyone before encoffinment gives family members a lot of closure and comfort. We also comb the deceased's eyebrows to make sure the hair is aligned in the same direction, and use eyeliner to darken the line where the eyelids meet. We use tools to flick out all of the eyelashes, some of which may be stuck inward, and apply mascara to darken white lashes. These are details that matter.

Once we have completed the embalming process and the deceased is presentable, we carefully place the body in a casket or onto a stretcher before it is loaded into the van to be brought to the venue of the wake.

One of the biggest misconceptions people have about embalming—it is sometimes the reason they choose not to embalm their loved ones—is that we cut open the body, remove the organs, and throw them away. We do not. The only time we have to open up the body is when we have to work on an autopsied case.

An autopsy takes place when people do not die of natural causes and a forensic pathologist is called in to ascertain the cause of death and the medical condition of the deceased. During an autopsy, if an internal examination is required, the forensic pathologist will examine all the internal organs, such as the heart, brain, and lungs, by weighing them and testing for the presence of chemicals. A Y-shaped cut will be made, with the two arms of the Y running down each shoulder joint to meet at the chest midway, and the stem of the Y running down to the pubic region. The chest plate will be removed with a saw or a rib cutter.

If a brain autopsy is required, the pathologist makes a cut across the crown of the head, from behind one ear to the other, before opening the cranium using a special saw.

Once the autopsy is complete, the organs are carefully placed back into the body, the skull is fitted back together and the skin is sewn shut.

When an autopsied body comes to us, we can't just proceed with embalming in the usual way. Many blood vessels would have been severed during the autopsy, and if we try to pipe in the embalming chemicals, it will not reach many areas of the body.

We thus have to embalm the organs separately. We undo the stitches along the Y-shaped cut down the front of the body, then remove the intestines, heart, lungs, stomach, liver, pancreas, and kidneys. In some other countries where I have done embalming, the forensic pathologist would place these organs into a bag before slipping them back into the cavity. This makes work much easier for the embalmers later. But in Singapore, the organs are laid back in the body cavity without being bagged.

We carefully extract the organs and place them in a double-layered bag, then pour embalming chemicals into the bag to let the organs soak. While they are soaking, we proceed to embalm the rest of the body. In the event that the chemicals do not reach a certain part of the body, given that blood vessels have been severed in the autopsy process, we have six points through which we can separately inject the chemicals: the femoral arteries in the left and right legs, the subclavian arteries through the left and right arms, and the left and right carotid arteries. After that, we dry the inside of the cavity and lay the bag of organs within. Finally, the Y incision is stitched up once more.

While the idea of embalming might turn the stomachs of some, I am not afraid of it. Embalming is actually one of my favorite parts of the job, for it is when I feel closest to the deceased. To me, those that I care for on the embalming table are benign people whom I am preparing for their last journey in life.

I talk to them as I work: "Auntie, please guide my hand and give me the ability to help you look good," or, "Uncle, we need to put in your dentures so you can look nice." It is my way of showing respect to my clients, even if they are dead.

The bodies come to us in different conditions, depending on how the person had died. Some, apart from having a few plasters placed over the punctures left behind by drips and injections, look like they are sleeping peacefully. Others who had been battling chronic illnesses like cancer, or who were wheelchair bound or bedridden for an extended period of time, may look emaciated. Their skin may be hanging off their bones and their cheeks may be sunken. They may also have lost their hair and eyelashes through aggressive chemotherapy treatments. These present extra challenges when they come to us to be embalmed.

We try, as best we can, to restore a healthy appearance to the body. If the deceased used to wear a wig, we get it from the family. For ladies who have lost their eyelashes to chemotherapy, we ask the family if they want us to apply false eyelashes. We can also place some stuffing in the mouth to plump up the cheeks, but we cannot go too far or the deceased might become unrecognizable.

Then there are those who die from burns—I have encountered two burn victims in the course of my work.

In the first case, in 2015, when I went to the Singapore General Hospital morgue, the deceased had been placed in a white body bag, which we at the funeral parlor never opened as the body had been burnt beyond recognition. There was nothing that embalming or cosmetics could have done. We transferred the bag into the casket, which was immediately brought to the Mandai crematorium for cremation.

The gentleman in the body bag was an Australian in his seventies who had been visiting Singapore for business. The house of his friend and business associate, at which he had been staying, had caught fire.

My second case, which occurred in 2016, was another household fire tragedy. This time, though, we could restore his appearance, despite the fact that he had suffered burns to over 70 percent of his body.

The fire occurred at about 5 am. While most of the occupants of the condominium unit had managed to escape, the patriarch, who was in his sixties, and who had been dragged out of his house alive by his son, later died in hospital. His wife also suffered burns to 24 percent of her body.

What we saw as we laid him on our embalming table was that his face was beetroot-red, as if he had suffered an extreme case of sunburn. His skin was mostly dry, although there were a few raw patches that were moist. He had suffered second-degree burns. The first layer of his skin had been burnt off, and what we were seeing was the second layer. There were also small black bits of charred flesh clinging to his skin.

We sloughed off the charred flesh and rigorously applied makeup. We had to paint over the redness with layers of beige creams and powders. We also had to apply the powder to the moist patches to dry them up. The process therefore took longer than usual, as we applied a layer of drying powder, then delicately applied the foundation.

Thankfully, his hair was intact. But we did have to spend some time filling in his eyebrows. Based on photographs that the family had supplied, we noticed that his distinguishing feature was a pair of bristly jet black eyebrows that might have been singed in the fire.

Everyone at the wake was aware he had died in the fire. Those who commented on his appearance were surprised at how he looked as he did in life, and it was reassuring for family and friends who wanted to see him for the last time.

There are also suicide and accident victims who may have suffered trauma if their deaths were violent, or who may be missing some parts of their bodies. The embalmer then has to reconstruct the damaged body parts. For a teenage accident victim who had lost part of her hair, leaving her scalp partially visible, the embalmers managed to conceal the portion by carefully placing and setting some hair over the spot.

In the hands of a professional embalmer, who is a bit of a surgeon, makeup artist, and craftsperson all rolled into one, the craft of embalming effectively provides the semblance of peaceful deep sleep to the dead.

CHAPTER 6

Jason's Smile

*T*he dead youth lying in front of me on the steel table reminded me of my brother—they were both lean young men in the prime of their lives.

Jason Lim—in my heart, I call my clients by name—now belonged to that category of people felled by acute death, or sudden death. Family members are more or less emotionally prepared for their loved one's death if it is caused by chronic diseases like cancer, and are sometimes even relieved that their loved one is no longer suffering. But unexpected deaths, caused by the likes of brain aneurysms, sudden cardiac arrests, suicides, or accidents, can have a catastrophic effect on families.

When he died in June 2010, Jason was a passenger in his father's grey multipurpose vehicle. They were making an early drive home to Muar after visiting relatives in Kuantan. Just before 7:45 am, as the car streaked along the expressway, a trailer truck going in the opposite direction swerved to the right to overtake a vehicle in front of it. There was no road divider, nothing to stop the trailer as it shot straight into the path of the multipurpose vehicle.

Jason, his father, two younger sisters, and grandmother died on the spot. His mother, one sister, and youngest brother survived, but were badly injured and had to be hospitalized. The driver of the trailer truck was only slightly injured. He was charged with reckless driving, which carries up to 10 years imprisonment and a fine of up to RM5,000[7] if convicted, but I never found out what the verdict was.

The Lims were based in Muar and were active in church. The patriarch was a respected vice-principal of a secondary school. His six children, whose ages ranged from 13 to 26 at the time of the accident, were likely a great source of parental pride as they were clean-cut and wholesome academic achievers. The eldest child, a daughter, was working in the UK at the time and was the only one not in the vehicle.

This is the sort of business no funeral director wants to get. Until now, their case has been one of the hardest I have ever worked on and I would consider it to be the one that prepared me for the rest of my career, not only due to the scale of the tragedy, but because I was relatively new to the profession at the time. For me, this was the deepest end of the pool, and I emerged with a profound sense of the impact that a funeral director can make.

At the time, I had just returned to the funeral industry after five years of working in financial services, during which I had occasionally helped my mother out with her funeral business. I had spent a year setting up TransLifeCare when the call came into my Malaysian business partner—a family of five had died in an accident. One of the victims, the grandmother, had pre-purchased a funeral plot with my partner's company, which was then asked to handle the funerals for the other four as well. I was tasked to organize the funeral for all five.

When the bodies were brought to the embalming facility in Kuala Lumpur, it was 4 am. It was then that I saw how

7 A little over $1000 USD.

embalmers could use their skills to transform the bodies of five people, all of whom had suffered injuries through the accident, almost to how they had looked in life. There were five of us on the embalming team, but rather than working on one body each, we worked as a group to care for each of the accident victims. Dressed from head to toe in blue scrubs, with our hair covered with plastic caps, we toiled for hours in the brightly lit embalming room that was fortunately large enough to accommodate all five bodies.

We removed their clothes and gently bathed each family member. Eyes and mouths that gaped had to be closed; the gas in a bloated abdomen had to be released through a careful incision that was then plugged with a special button; a broken limb where the blood vessels had been severed had to be embalmed via hypodermic injections of embalming fluid directly into the affected vessels; plasters and special makeup were liberally applied to restore their appearances.

There was little we could do for the two teenage girls as water retention and bloating had rendered their faces unrecognizable despite our best efforts. The decision was made to cover their faces with sheer white handkerchiefs.

Jason had sustained an odious head injury that had ripped off part of his scalp. Multiple cuts marred his face. Because he reminded me of my brother, seeing him was particularly grim and, amongst the five, he was the toughest for me to embalm. We had to close up the skin on his scalp, and applied wax to reconstruct part of it. It was a tough job, like trying to repair a broken doll. In my heart, I quietly told him, "I really need to make you look good."

The moment of reckoning was when the relatives took their first looks at the embalmed bodies. While little was said, I could see in their faces that they were comforted. I then realized that one of the most meaningful things a funeral director can do for a family is to properly embalm their loved ones and present them as they had appeared when they were alive.

The bodies were then brought back to Muar, a one-and-a-half-hour drive away, for a church funeral where a whole new set of challenges loomed.

Because this was a funeral for five, I had to think hard about how to manage the logistics and make all the arrangements, from trying to procure enough hearses to transport the caskets—few companies would have had five hearses on hand—to managing the flow of visitors.

For instance, it was difficult to arrange five caskets in a room to ensure a smooth flow of people. I wanted to arrange the caskets around the perimeter of the room, so that visitors could come in, walk round to each of the caskets, then exit from where they had come in. But the worker from the church where the wake was being held insisted on an H-shaped arrangement, with one casket between two pairs. There would be no clear route for the visitors.

He pushed his point, and I shoved right back.

I said firmly, "This is not an exhibition; this is a funeral. Have you ever handled a funeral for five? How can you do an H-shape? I cannot control the flow of visitors if you use this sort of arrangement, and it will be difficult for me to stop the media from sneaking in to take photographs."

He shouted back in Hokkien, "You cannot do it your way!"

I explained the situation to Jason's uncle and aunt, who were the family members in charge of the funeral arrangements. They agreed with me, although the church worker was not happy.

I also decided to station four workers at the entrance of the room to block the view from the outside. The accident made great tabloid fodder. Grisly photographs of the accident scene had already been splashed in the newspapers, and reporters, photographers, and videographers had been lurking around the lobby of the funeral parlor trying to ferret out information for the next day's headlines. I was especially concerned about members of the media sneaking in to steal shots of the bodies, or surreptitiously accosting unprepared family members for interviews.

I understood that the media had to do their job. But my priorities were clear. From attending funeral talks in Australia and New Zealand, I learned that the job of a funeral director is not limited to organizing a funeral, but is also to protect the family members. Up until then, I had never organized a funeral in which the media were interested. But when I am unsure, I rely on my instincts—if I were in the family's shoes, what would I want the funeral director to do?

I decided to speak politely and rationally to the reporters and photographers when they arrived at the funeral home. They were lurking around in the lobby, waiting for the family to arrive. I informed the family to call us when they reached so that we could bring them in from the backdoor. In order to contain the reporters and photographers, I invited them away from the lobby to a room on the second floor. This session took place before the bodies had been brought to the church. There were about 10 of them, and I didn't think it would be wise to antagonize them or shoo them away. Instead, I appealed to their sense of humanity: "Have you lost someone before? You know it's painful losing one family member—now imagine losing five, with three more still in the hospital's intensive care unit. I am sure all of you can relate to that. This is not an easy time for them."

I proposed meeting them at 6 pm every day. They could tell me what angles their editors wanted, whom they wanted to interview, and I would relay their wishes to the family. If the family were agreeable, they would be interviewed in a separate room. It would also save the family members from the hassle of being asked the same questions *ad nauseam*. The reporters and photographers agreed.

One of the relatives requested that I sit in on the interviews. I said yes and assured him, "If at any point you feel that the questions are too sensitive, and you don't want to answer, just look at me and I'll help."

However, the family did not want to be photographed. People who are grieving do not look their best. They also did not want secret shots of the funeral to be published.

I learned how to engage the media when possible, but my priority is always the family. In Singapore in 2012, a Japanese woman was in a taxi when a speeding Ferrari crashed into it, and her wake was held at my father's funeral parlor. The funeral attracted a lot of media attention but the family was unprepared for it. When I saw that photographers were using zoom lenses to take photographs of the funeral proceedings from afar, I ordered my staff to block the view of the entrance of the parlor by lining three vans up in front of it, and to place potted plants to block the gaps between the vans.

For the Lims' funerals, my engagement strategy with the Malaysian media proved effective. Apart from one instance of a flash going off as the caskets were being unloaded from the hearse into the funeral parlor—I asked that the photo be deleted—the media respectfully surrendered their cameras as they approached the entrance to the hall. Upon my request, the newspapers even agreed to publish a bank account number so that members of the public could donate funds directly to the family.

While I did not want the media to take photos, the family asked me to photograph the bodies privately because Jason's mother, who was paralyzed from the neck down, his 14-year-old sister and 11-year-old brother were lying in the intensive care unit at a Kuantan hospital. They were not able to attend the funeral but they needed to see their family members in their final repose.

We filmed a video that they watched later. With the hymn "Amazing Grace" as the soundtrack, the video started with the opening of a set of doors into a room where the five bodies were placed on the embalming tables, after which the camera panned over each individual's photo, their face, and finally their body.

Aside from having to manage the media, crowd control was an issue. There were many visitors because there were five deaths and Jason's father was a well-loved educator. On the day of the funeral, a huge number of people gathered to pay their respects, including hordes of students coming in on chartered buses that were parked along the road. As the people milled about, blocking the only lane leading into the church where the wake was being held, one of the volunteers shouted into her microphone, "All of you stand behind me! The funeral director needs to do something, I don't know what, ah, so you all just stand behind me."

There wasn't much that could be done about the size of the crowd, but it could have been managed more sensitively. I quickly took over the microphone and said, "Ladies and gentlemen, as we begin the funeral procession, I ask for your cooperation to move aside so that we can conduct a dignified send-off for all of them. Thank you for your understanding."

It was a moment where I had to ad lib, but at a funeral of this nature, where there had been no precedent, no instructions in a training manual or a mentor who could guide me, I had to put the family first and then use my common sense. There were people who wanted to be photographed donating checks or rendering assistance to the family, expecting these photos to be published in the newspapers together with articles praising their generosity. I made sure that the family did not have to entertain unnecessary requests in their difficult time. I may have offended some people in the process, but they were not my priority.

However, I did have to wrestle with my own emotions in coping with the case. I realized that organizing funerals for a living doesn't make you immune to grief, especially if you can relate to the deceased in some way.

During the wake, Jason's family members told me many funny, happy stories about him that they would first laugh at, then cry over. I learned he had been a talented musician who could play the guitar, bass guitar, drums, and piano. He had been the prankster of the family, and his sense of humor had always been apparent in photos of him, where he had always exhibited a pair of deep dimples when he smiled. I was told he had been a month away from graduating from university.

I managed to keep my emotions in check until Jason's frail grandfather came to the wake in a wheelchair. Once the old man reached the entrance of the room where the coffins had been placed, he tried to stand up. Helping hands came from all sides to support him as he hobbled, painfully and slowly, to each of the caskets. When he reached Jason, the old man cried out in Mandarin, "Weren't you going to introduce your girlfriend to Ah Gong [grandfather]?"

What he said broke my heart and I could not help but cry. Some of the men working at the funeral stared at me in consternation. "How can you be a funeral director if you are so emotional?" The family members who were there offered me their tissues. Despite my tears, I remembered how my mother had swallowed her grief to attend to clients on the day of my father's funeral, and I continued doing my job in guiding the family.

I may be a funeral director, but I am also human. I often tell my staff: The day you stop feeling sadness for the family is the day you lose empathy and compassion, which is needed to work well in my company because we have to go the extra mile for families.

It is also important for the family to show their emotions and cry. Jason's eldest sibling flew back from the UK to help organize the funeral. She was unemotional when she did what she had to do, such as opening a bank account for public donations to her family and greeting those who came to the funeral to pay their respects. When other people became upset at the wake, she hugged and consoled them. She did not want to see the bodies of her family or go near the caskets. She said she wanted to remember them as they were when they were alive.

I was concerned. I had learned in my funeral studies that viewing the dead body and saying goodbye are necessary for emotional closure, and it is not normal for a person whose family has been decimated to not shed a single tear. One of my acquaintances had once told me that her biggest regret was not being able to see her father as he lay in his casket because her relatives had not allowed her to. They had mistakenly thought that she had been too young.

It is for this reason that it is very difficult—in situations where a person is presumed dead, but where their body has never been recovered—for their loved ones to come to terms with his death. They might never be fully convinced that their loved one is really dead. A couple, whose son had most likely died during the September 11 terrorist attacks that took place in New York in 2001, had buried some of his personal belongings as a formality, but they could never walk past the former site of the World Trade Center buildings without scrutinizing the faces of the homeless people there, hoping against hope that their son might have amnesia and might perhaps be among them.

So I was somewhat relieved when, on the day of the Muar funeral, after the rest of the family had said their last goodbyes and just as the caskets were being readied to be moved into the hearses, the daughter came to me and asked quietly, "I would like to see my family. Do we have the time?"

I told her, "Take all the time you need. We will not leave until you are ready."

She slowly said goodbye to each of her family members. When she came to her two sisters, the tears finally fell. But she stayed calm throughout. She told me later, "I cannot afford to break down. I still have to take care of my mother and two other siblings." I put my arm around her shoulder and gave her a comforting squeeze.

Some funerals are so devastating that the sadness never quite goes away. In the aftermath of the Lims' funeral, I retreated to Singapore, physically, mentally, and emotionally exhausted. I had worked for 96 hours on the funeral with little sleep, and needed three days to recover.

Three years after the funeral, I received a message from Jason's aunt, the one who had made the funeral arrangements with me. The 11-year-old boy who had survived the accident, and who had been in and out of hospital since then, had succumbed to complications and died.

I once had a dream about Jason. Most dreams float away upon waking, but I remember clearly that in this dream, he smiled at me, his dimples flashing.

CHAPTER 7

Death by One's Own Hand

S ome people in South Korea have been pretending to die and holding mock funerals for themselves. The organizers of such death experience programs hope that the participants will do some soul-searching and rethink the value of their lives. The greater aim is to address and hopefully bring down the nation's suicide rate, which is considered one of the highest in the developed world.

The 2016 statistics from the World Health Organization put South Korea's suicide rate at 20.2 suicides per 100,000 people per year, which is the highest in Asia. Guyana's suicide rate of 30.2 suicides per 100,000 people per year is the highest in the world. According to the Seoul Suicide Prevention Center, about 43 people take their own lives every day in South Korea. Singapore's suicide rate is much lower, ranked 97 globally, with a suicide rate of 7.4 suicides per 100,000 people per year.

Mock funerals, which were pioneered by the Hyowon Healing Center in Seoul, cater to those who are struggling in their lives, including teenagers who are battling exam stress in the pressure-cooker academic environment, and older people who fear becoming a financial burden on their families.

At one such "mass funeral" in Seoul, the participants wrote wills and farewell letters. They watched inspirational videos of how others, like cancer sufferers, overcame adversity and made the choice to bravely continue living. Then they climbed into caskets as a man dressed in black, representing the "Angel of Darkness," closed the lids. They stayed in their "tombs" for 10 minutes where they contemplated their lives, the lives of those they would leave behind, and their afterlives. Many were moved to tears when they realized how much pain they would cause their loved ones if they were to die.

The Yeouido Water Rescue Unit is a team responsible for rescuing the people who leap from Seoul's Mapo Bridge, one of the most popular spots in the city at which to attempt suicide. The team studies CCTV footage, looks out for people who are behaving suspiciously and sometimes rushes to haul people out of the water after they have jumped.

In Singapore, suicide numbers fluctuated from 361 in 2011, to 467 in 2012, and 397 in 2018. However, there has been a jump in the number of those aged 60 and above ending their own lives, from 79 in 2000 to 126 in 2014, as well as that of young people. In 2015, 27 youngsters aged between 10 and 19 killed themselves—twice as many as the year before. This was the highest in 15 years. According to Samaritans of Singapore (SOS),[8] suicide is the leading cause of death for those aged 15 to 29. Many who called the organization for help said they were facing mental health issues, academic or work pressure, and relationship problems at home, school, or the workplace.

Interestingly, another trend in the past decade has been that the number of men committing suicide has risen by nearly 30 percent, while suicides by women have fallen by 20 percent. In

8 The Samaritans of Singapore (SOS) is a 24-hour non-profit suicide prevention center. It can be reached at 1800 221 4444 and www.sos.org.sg.

2018, men accounted for more than 71 percent of all suicides in Singapore. An expert quoted in a July 2015 news article suggested that this could be because men feel compelled to solve their own problems in isolation and suppress feelings of distress due to traditional gender roles and stereotypes, while women are more likely to seek help. Notable male celebrities who have committed suicide include American comedian and actor Robin Williams, as well as celebrity chef, author, and documentarian Anthony Bourdain.

Globally, the Covid-19 pandemic, which struck the world in 2020, has caused people to take their own lives. A top New York-based emergency room doctor, Dr. Lorna Breen, had been treating coronavirus patients before she killed herself in April 2020. Her father, who said she had contracted Covid-19 and recovered before going back to work, added that she was devastated by the toll the virus was taking on patients. With the global population suffering from work, financial, and domestic woes, it may result in even more suicides from people who feel that life is not worth living.

The Singapore government has shifted its approach towards suicide. In the past, attempting to take one's own life was a crime in Singapore, punishable by fines or up to one year in jail. To get a sense of how prevalent this is, out of 1,096 cases of attempted suicide in 2015, 837 people were arrested.

But in late 2018, it was recommended by a special committee that those who attempted suicide should not be put on trial under the criminal justice system. They need treatment, not prosecution, and their act should not be considered a crime but a cry for help.

Just how many attempts are there? The SOS estimates that for every suicide, there are at least six suicide survivors left behind; meaning that for 397 suicides in 2017, there might have been at least 2,300 others who did not succeed in killing themselves.

Government agencies focus on suicide prevention and offering a helping hand to those in emotional distress. They work quietly together in the early detection and prevention of potential suicide cases, give talks to students on mental health issues and provide social support to the elderly who may be depressed. It is a quiet effort because suicide is still stigmatized in Singapore, and not something that most people are willing to talk about. The press conscientiously avoids covering suicide cases out of fear of inspiring copycats, and will only do so if there is a newsworthy element.

When I am called to deal with a death, I immediately know that it is a suicide when the death certificate states that the location of the death is at the void deck. Jumping from a high-rise flat or the corridor of a block of flats is a fairly common mode of suicide in Singapore. In my line of work, I have also had to deal with those who have hanged themselves.

In one instance, I received a telephone call from a friend of the family. "Hello, Angjolie, my friend needs your help. His father has just killed himself and my friend doesn't know what to do," the man on the other end of the line said. Usually in Singapore, whenever a suicide occurs, the friends or family of the deceased should also call 999, as the police have to determine if any foul play is involved.

I immediately rushed down to the address I had been given. The old man's son opened the door. "Ms. Ang, it's you! I saw you on TV!" (I had recently been featured in a television program about funerals.) He continued, "I'm so happy it was you who came." I was astounded by the cheerful reception. It was also slightly surreal to see mother and son pottering about the house, calmly going about their business. Perhaps the reality of the man's death had not quite sunk in.

I asked to see the old man. I was brought to his bedroom and there I saw his body, still hanging from the curtain railing, with his tongue sticking out. There was a stool on the floor that looked like it had been knocked over—the man had probably been standing on it earlier. I also saw that the son had lit two candles and put them next to his father, and had switched on a recording of Buddhist chants.

The son asked, "Can I take him down?"

"No," I told him. "You can't touch anything in the room and you can't touch his body. We need to call the police."

Eight police officers soon arrived. One of the policemen, armed with a battery of questions, sat down with the matriarch. He asked her, "When did you last see him alive? What were you doing when you discovered the body? How did you discover him? Where was your son when you found your husband?" Once he had finished, another policeman took up the vacated seat and asked similar questions—then another policeman, and another.

I quietly took one of the officers aside and asked him, "Why are you all asking her the same questions?"

He replied, "We want to make sure her story is consistent. By the way, could you stay with the wife for a while? We don't want her to kill herself too." It is apparently not uncommon for a spouse, who cannot accept the death of their partner, to take their life as well.

Subsequently, a post-mortem was conducted, as is required in suicide cases, to establish that no foul play had been involved. I later found out that the patriarch had killed himself to spare his family from having to bear the financial burden of his medical bills as he had recently been diagnosed with cancer.

The morning of his suicide, the old couple's only son had left for work as usual while the old lady had headed to the market. Before she left, she had knocked on their bedroom door, which was locked, and had asked her husband, "Do you want food?" He had impatiently brushed her off. "Don't bother me!" Those were probably his last words.

When she returned home, the bedroom door was still locked. After knocking on it several times without getting any response, she felt that something was amiss. She called her son, who then rushed home and, as he was unable to locate the room key, broke down the door.

After the funeral, the family gave us a box of macarons to thank us. Sometimes I get gifts from my clients as tokens of appreciation. The mother also gave me a teardrop-shaped pearl pendant, as she said she did not want me to ever forget her. She was touched at how we had given her husband a dignified send-off.

Sadly, this was not the first time I had encountered such a case, nor would it be the last. When the elderly kill themselves, it is often because they do not want to be a burden to their families.

I recalled the policeman's instructions—for me to stay with the wife lest she kill herself—when I later attended to a double suicide. A man had jumped to his death in the early morning. When the police went up to his residence to inform his wife, she went to the kitchen window, looked down and saw her husband's body lying below. Without a second thought, she took off after him. They were both aged 48 and did not have children. I understood from their family members that the husband, who worked in the private sector, had lost his job and had fallen into a deep depression. The couple was very close. As the husband grew more and more despondent, he might have felt that life's journey was too bleak for him to carry on. She might have felt that she could not go on without him.

Amongst those left behind were each of their mothers, two amongst the many visitors packed into the crematorium hall, who had to suffer the anguish of living with the fact that their children had chosen to end their lives.

As a new mother myself, my life would go dark if my child were ever to kill herself, which was why I was struck when I read a book by Linda Collins, *Loss Adjustment*, which depicted how she picked up the pieces of her life after her daughter Victoria committed suicide. It is a long, hard journey which never ends.

A group of mothers in Singapore whose children had committed suicide came together to form a support group called PleaseStay to help other parents cope with the emotional trauma. Four of the mothers, who gave video interviews to speak candidly about their personal experiences, said they hoped that the group would be a catalyst for change by advocating mental wellness and suicide prevention amongst youths. I think the support from those who have had the same experience is timely, and puts the spotlight on a subject that has traditionally been taboo and only whispered about.

The subject of children committing suicide hit closer to home when I helped out with the funeral of a 12-year-old boy. After taking his Primary School Leaving Examination (PSLE), a high-stakes national assessment, he received his results. I did not know what his results were, but good or bad performance is often extremely subjective. The fact is that he responded by jumping off a block of flats. It is not the first time a Singaporean child has committed suicide over academic results, as stress from academic performance is a pressure point for children and youths, who may not know how to express their fears. He was an only child.

The family wanted to get the funeral over and done with, quietly and quickly. So quickly that the embalmer did not have the time to patch the boy's skull—a technical exercise of carefully using cable ties to secure the pieces of bone together. It would have taken many hours. Still, the power of reconstruction is in giving family members a greater degree of closure, which was unfortunately absent during the funeral.

Both parents were devastated, the mother wailing, the father quiet in a corner with tears in his eyes. At one point, the father shouted at his wife, "Can you stop crying?" Perhaps they felt guilty and blamed themselves, or each other.

Younger suicide victims most likely kill themselves because they are suffering from depression. Between 2012 and 2013, statistics captured in Singapore showed that suicides involving those between 20 and 29 years old registered a significant increase. In 2018, 94 young people took their own lives, and suicide was unfortunately the leading cause of death for those aged 10 to 29.

In the case of the double suicide, I was given a deeper glimpse into the illness when a family decided that the funeral was a platform to raise awareness of the condition and to address its perils—that depression is not just something in one's mind that can be overcome by strength of will; it is a severe illness that can destroy lives.

I once attended to the death of a 25-year-old student from India who had come to Singapore to study. She had hanged herself in her hostel room. Her parents flew over in the morning and we had a very short ceremony for their only child before her body was flown back on a 2 am flight the next day. They were in a hurry to get her home.

After getting the embalming and sealing certificate—as well as her passport, death certificate, and police report—we obtained an export permit from the Indian embassy. Her casket was wrapped up tightly in black plastic before being placed in a crate.

Her parents called me the next morning after they had arrived in India to thank me personally, and to tell me that her body was still in good condition.

On a personal note, whenever I come across a suicide case, it weighs heavily on my mind. What would possibly compel a person to take their own life? Do they know how their family and friends would grieve for the sudden and unexplainable loss? And do they know how guilty everyone around them would feel for not picking up the signs?

Because there is that one troubling aspect about suicides: Sometimes, people can't tell if someone is going to do it. There are no signs and symptoms.

As a funeral director, I felt that same guilt when one of our clients killed herself. To make me feel worse, she had even prepared herself very well for it—with my company.

Marianne came to us to pre-plan her funeral. This is called a pre-need service, which is for people who want to plan in advance while they are still alive on how their funeral should be conducted, so that their loved ones won't have to cope with the extra burden. We walked through her options, arranged everything, and put it down on paper. She even made payment. Shortly after, the 40-year-old killed herself.

It was a case that haunted me: Why didn't we—as deathcare "professionals"—spot the signs? And why didn't her family members, who would have spent more time with her, have any clue as to what was going through her mind?

When Marianne came to us, she was cheery and behaved as normally as any other passerby. She was in a marketing job, married with no children, and first made contact with us through email. She was keen to find out more about our initiative to combine human ashes with soil in a biodegradable pot, into which we place a plant that can grow over the years.

In hindsight, we should have picked up on what was a fairly unusual scenario and tried to drill a little deeper into the reasons she wanted to think about her funeral.

While I advocate planning for your funeral way in advance—and I have done so myself—the reality is that most people who do so are either older or chronically sick. Few are young, hale, and hearty, like Marianne. She had the demeanor of a girl-next-door, with a bright, sweet smile and a shoulder-length bob. It was also strange that, while she was married, she did not want to involve her husband in the discussions.

She met my teammates twice to run through the very detailed things she would have to consider—like type of coffin, her final apparel, how she would want to customize her funeral, even her makeup. She sent us a photo of a model, showing the kind of simple, natural makeup she wanted. At no point in our dealings was there any sign of the terrible thing she was contemplating. In the email where she had attached a picture of the final outfit she wanted to wear in her coffin, she had even written, "This might change according to my preferences as the years go by."

After the discussions, what we do is outline all the instructions and give the client a customized pre-need card containing their policy number and personal details. It serves to inform family members that the cardholder has arranged their funeral plans with us.

The bombshell dropped on the very day we were supposed to mail out the pre-need card to Marianne.

It was truly ironic that it came in the form of a call to my mobile phone at the moment my finger was poised over the doorbell of the SOS office at Cantonment Close, where I was scheduled to have a meeting. I was supposed to have a discussion with the SOS about how to reach out to people and dissuade them from committing suicide.

"Hi, are you Angjolie? Do you have a client by the name of Marianne?"

These were the cold words that trickled down my spine and froze me in my tracks. Over the phone, Marianne's friend informed me that she had passed away, and asked if I could go down to meet the family right away.

I was in a state of shock and disbelief. What had happened?

There were no clear answers forthcoming even when we met the family at the activity room of Marianne's condominium. Her husband was wailing beyond control and was inconsolable. He was the one who had found her, dead by carbon monoxide poisoning, when he came home that morning.

But what we gathered was that there had been marital issues. While he appeared grief-stricken, her husband had apparently had an affair.

Even as I grappled with the "whys," her family members, too, were equally devastated without any answers. In the cruel echo of hindsight, they realized the only clue she gave away was when she handed over her insurance documents to her parents the night before she killed herself, informing them to pass it to her sister. She said nothing to her parents, who recalled that she behaved normally; they did not notice anything amiss.

Her family had no idea Marianne had consulted a funeral director. They only knew of my existence after the police found her pre-need plan folder in her apartment with my name card in it.

They turned to me for answers: "Did she say anything? What was she like when she talked to you?" My answers did not provide them any clues. My team and I could not help but feel somewhat responsible for her death.

The funeral went exactly the way she planned it. She had likely considered the possibility that her family would have found it very difficult to organize. She was clad in a simple white dress, and her face looked natural, the way she wanted it. Her wake was held at the void deck of her parent's HDB flat that she grew up in, and was adorned with canvases of her artwork—she was a recreational artist. One of her biggest artworks featured two peacocks, with these words from the Bible: "Love is patient. Love is kind. Love never gives up, never loses faith, is always hopeful, and endures through every circumstance" (1 Cor. 13:7 New Living Translation).

As a steady procession of her many friends visited the funeral, they listened to the pop tunes she had chosen, like "A Thousand Years" by Christina Perri and "Cups" by Anna Kendrick, with its now-poignant lyrics—"You're gonna miss me when I'm gone."

When it was time for us to send her to the crematorium, Marianne's father had to be helped by six people. They surrounded him, propping him up. His face was full of tears and mucus and his spectacles were askew as he tried to grab my hand and begged me not to take her today. My heart broke at the thought of this white-haired gentleman having to bid farewell to his black-haired, beloved youngest daughter, and I had to struggle to hold back my tears. His grief is the real face of suicide and its impact on those left behind. On its website, the SOS has a list of warning signs to help recognize suicidal ideation. These include verbal warnings, like a person saying, "life is too painful for me," pre-suicide planning that may include researching methods of dying, and emotional or behavioral changes such as intense feelings of rage or hopelessness. Through my work, I have learned to be more sensitive to those around me who may need help. We may be the ones to provide a reason for someone else to keep on living.

Do keep a lookout. By the time I get there, it's too late.

CHAPTER 8

Bringing Daddy Home

*F*or two months in 2012, the body of the old gentleman lay unclaimed, unidentified, in cold storage in the morgue of the Singapore General Hospital. Until he died, he was but an anonymous wrinkled elder, one of nearly 50,000 senior citizens in Singapore who live their twilight years in solitude.

Sadly, their numbers are set to increase as the Department of Statistics estimates that 83,000 elderly persons will be living alone by 2030.

Uncle was found lying dead on the floor of his HDB flat, clad in a worn-out singlet and shorts, which he continued wearing throughout his stay at the morgue.

It took the hospital nearly two months to locate Uncle's family members. He had three daughters—one of them was married to a Christian pastor whom I had worked with at an earlier funeral, who remembered me and picked up the phone to call me.

He said, "Angjolie, I need your help. We just found out that my father-in-law has passed away, but we have not been in contact with him for years. Can you help to arrange for a straight cremation?"

"May I know when we can transfer your father-in-law into our care?"

"Any time tomorrow."

"May I then suggest that we have the cremation tomorrow afternoon? This will give us ample time to bathe, dress, and prepare him in the morning before the Cremation."

The next morning, having booked a 3 pm cremation slot at the Mandai Crematorium, we brought Uncle from SGH to our Care Center at around 11 am.

There was no need for embalming, as his body was not required to last for several days and would be cremated by mid-afternoon. Even then, I strongly believe that for everybody that we serve, the barest minimum we should do is to bathe the body, shampoo his hair, close his eyes and mouth, comb his hair, and at least let the deceased look peaceful and presentable.

But as my able Filipina decedent care assistant, Chelo, and I suited up and put on our gloves and surgical masks, we knew we had our work cut out for us even though we weren't required to exchange his blood with embalming fluids.

Uncle had probably been found before his body was in an advanced state of decay. However, his body had been lying in a fridge for two months and, while the cold environment had slowed down the rate of decomposition drastically, his skin had been dehydrated. His head was tilted and loose, like a puppet whose internal string connecting its head and body had been severed.

I had to set Uncle's head straight. Then we had to set his features. There is a Chinese proverb—死不瞑目, *si bu ming mu*— that refers to someone who had died with his eyes open but, on a deeper level, means that the person had not died peacefully.

In Chinese movies or TV shows, the classic scene in such cases of death is of a hand passing over the face to close the eyelids, as if that would bring about emotional closure for the person who had died. Uncle's eyes were wide open. Was it because he had died a traumatic death? Or was it because he had died with unresolved conflicts? In reality, neither of these would have had anything to do with why his eyes were open. Even if one dies with closed eyes, the eyes of the deceased will gradually open as the slackened eyelids fall back. Unless something is done to keep them closed, the eyes of every dead person will gradually open after a few hours, as the muscles that keep the eyelids closed no longer work. In fact, it would be impossible to close the eyes by merely brushing a hand over the eyelids; it actually requires proper technique. Because the muscles stop working, the jaw also slackens and the mouth falls open. So without proper measures taken, no one who is dead would look like they are resting in peace. In the past, people resorted to some rather odd ways to defeat nature, like using a strip of cloth to tie a ribbon from the chin over the head to close the mouth, or even resorting to taping the eyes shut. However, these methods damage the skin of the deceased.

These days, if someone dies at home, I usually advise family members to place damp cotton wool over the eyelids, and roll up a towel to place under the chin of their loved one.

Chelo and I first took a shaver to Uncle's unkempt gray stubble. Liberal amounts of special peach-colored spray for the deceased helped to moisturize his skin, which months in the freezer had rendered as dry and tough as leather.

We then had to work on his eyes. They were not only open, but also sunken—the orbs were shrunken and shriveled due to the loss of fluids. We rolled up some cotton wool and placed it in the eye sockets to pad up the eye area, used tools to lift the eyelids, then inserted special flesh-colored eye caps that covered the front of the eyeball and shored up the structure. As these are imported from the US, they are sometimes a tad too big for Asian eyes. We trimmed them to fit Uncle's eyes.

To keep the eyelids in place, the caps are coated with a special adhesive cream. The surface of the caps is also studded with tiny textured triangular cutouts, so once the eyelid closes over the cap, it catches on the "barbs" and will no longer open. Lastly, we carefully hooked out eyelashes that had been stuck under the lids. Now he looked like he was sleeping.

Then came the smile. The cream, which works to keep the eyelids shut, is not strong enough for the jaw, which is heavier. To close the jaw, Chelo armed herself with a semi-circular needle and a length of 1mm-thick white suture string.

With the needle, she threaded the string through the bottom of his chin, through to the jaw below the gums. Then she stuck the string through the upper jaw into the right nostril, through the septum of the nose into the left nostril, and then passed it back down into the mouth. She tightened this string "pulley" to close the mouth and tied the two ends of the suture, leaving what appeared as a small dimple on the fleshy underside of his face, behind the chin.

However, the smile just didn't look right, even after a second attempt.

At times like these, we talk to the deceased. Chelo whispered, before making her adjustments, "Uncle, please guide my hand so that I can close your mouth nicely, and you can look your best for your family."

As she made her adjustments, hooks, lines, bones, and flesh eventually fell into place. Uncle looked like he was sleeping peacefully, with a slight smile on his face. "Thank you, Uncle," she murmured.

We removed the old singlet and trousers, dressed him in a Hawaiian print shirt and long pants that his daughters had provided, and gently arranged his hands to rest on his abdomen. We placed Uncle in a white casket and brought him to the Mandai Crematorium.

Uncle's three daughters and their husbands met us there. The last time they had seen him was when he was lying in the hospital morgue, with his eyes and mouth gaping wide. The pastor had been concerned then, as he did not want his wife and sisters-in-law to undergo the trauma of seeing their father that way again. I assured him, "Your father-in-law is presentable now; we have already cared for him."

Relieved, he beckoned his wife over. The moment she saw her father, peaceful in repose, her knees buckled and she had to brace herself on the side of the casket. Her daughter, the old man's granddaughter, supported her mother's weight, but she was herself sobbing. At this, the pastor turned to me and suggested, "We shall have a closed casket ceremony. We won't open it for the funeral."

But after the service, just before the casket was supposed to go into the incinerator for the cremation, Uncle's two other daughters asked to take one last look at their father. I glanced at the pastor and he nodded.

Two of my team members then opened the casket for them, and the daughters gathered around for their final farewells. As they gazed at their father, I wondered what was going through their minds. Did they think back to why they had fallen out with him? Would they have wanted to reconcile with him earlier?

No words were said, but the silence was broken by sniffles and then sobbing as all three women broke down. Even though they had been estranged from him, they still loved him.

Later, the sisters walked over and, one after the other, hugged me. "We had no idea you could make such a big difference," they said. "You really made our father look so much better than when we last saw him in the morgue."

It is odd, but sometimes death can bring families together. Before 1961, when polygamy became illegal in Singapore, some men had more than one wife. There are also families with children born out of wedlock, or blended families where people divorce and remarry. The various family members may not be on talking terms—they may even hate each other—but when someone in common with the two (or more) families dies, they sometimes all come together to grieve.

At a funeral for a man who had two families, on one side was his wife and daughter, and on the other side was his mistress who had borne him a daughter and a son. After he had fallen ill, both families had taken turns to care for him. And during the funeral, as the deceased was about to be cremated, his two daughters started crying. Then to my great surprise, the half-sisters hugged each other. I was later told that the two families eventually made peace.

CHAPTER 9

Keeping a Death Secret

hat is it like to have a loved one die and have to keep that fact a secret to protect the living? In late September 2016, a woman called me with an unusual question. Her husband had been found dead due to myocardial infarction.

She asked calmly, "My son is going to have his PSLE next week—do you think I should let him know about his father's death? We are also considering having the funeral back in my husband's hometown, Malacca. What should I do?"

The PSLE is a national examination that all Singaporean children have to sit for at the end of their primary school education. Most parents take it very seriously, as their child would need to do well to qualify for a good secondary school. This mother was torn between telling her son the news about his father's death before his examinations and risking the possibility that the emotional devastation would wreak havoc on his performance, or delaying disclosure until after the examinations, which would last about one and a half weeks.

When she called me, her husband's body was due to be collected the next day, after the post-mortem procedure. The usual practice in Singapore is that the body would be collected by the funeral director after the post-mortem procedure, the wake conducted immediately on the same day and the funeral a few days later. I felt it was crucial that the funeral be delayed, given her concern for her son. It would also give her time to gather her thoughts and mull over her options, particularly since the funeral might have to be held in Malaysia. I replied, "Would you be open to organizing your husband's funeral after your son's PSLE? You could seek the understanding of the police investigation officer and the Singapore General Hospital to keep your husband's body in the mortuary for another two weeks."

Both the officer and the hospital agreed. The body had to be kept at the mortuary as local funeral service providers, including us, do not have any cold storage facilities.

I met her twice to discuss the funeral arrangements. On one occasion, she had just dropped her son off at his tuition class and was meeting me while waiting for the boy—who must have been busy preparing for his examination—to finish. To the boy's questions about why his father was absent, she told him, "Daddy is ill in hospital. But he wants you to study hard for the exam and not get distracted."

The first time I saw her face-to-face, she appeared weary. I discovered that the woman, who was in her forties, had not been able to sleep at night. On top of working at her day job and helping her son to prepare for his exams, she did not have anyone to help her with the household chores. But she was determined to stay strong for her son and, apart from appearing fatigued, there was nothing in her demeanor that gave away the fact that she was putting on a monumental performance of leading a normal life while grappling with the death of her spouse and furtively organizing a funeral. While she had informed her own parents about her husband's death, she had not told her mother-in-law who was living in Malaysia, as the old lady was in ill health.

She decided to have her husband cremated in Singapore and to hold a memorial service in Malacca. To save her the hassle of having to engage a second funeral service provider in Malaysia, I contacted my funeral director partner in Malaysia to ensure that the transfer of the cremains and administrative paperwork would be handled seamlessly.

It was at the end of our first meeting that she asked the question that must have been weighing heavily on her mind: "How should I break the news to my son?"

I suggested she could use a memorial board that I would provide. "Families use this to come together and share their fondest memories of their loved one," I said. "After you have broken the news to him, do encourage him to share his feelings, cry together, talk about how his father made an impact on him, and what he would like to give his father."

On the last day of the PSLE in early October, I messaged her to ask how she was doing. The reply came late that night: "I have just completed the memorial board with my son."

The next day, after my staff and I had collected and embalmed the body, I saw the boy. He appeared calm and was with his mother at the Ang Yew Seng Remembrance Hall, the parlor where his father's funeral was being held. Taking pride of place at the entrance of the hall was the memorial board that mother and son had put together. The hall was teeming with nearly 70 people, and even as the mother greeted the guests and the boy sat down quietly in a corner with his grandmother, the queue to pay respects and view the body grew longer.

I suggested that the woman and her son should say farewell privately. I accompanied them as they approached the casket with a bag in hand. When they reached the casket, they drew out several items to place inside it. One was a drawing by the boy with the words "I love my Dad," and some wooden craft items that the boy appeared to have made himself. As his mother gazed upon her husband's face for the last time, I finally saw her cry. The boy, however, appeared somewhat dazed and unsure of how to express himself. Full awareness might only dawn on him later. After the cremation, the cremains were delivered straight to Malacca that afternoon.

What I remember most vividly from that funeral was the woman's fortitude—as a wife, she wanted to grieve for her dead husband, but as a mother, her grief took second place to her love for her son. Four years on, I caught up with the lady. She told me it was hard going at first, but her son has matured and grown to become the "man of the household," instinctively looking out for his mother.

I attended to another funeral where I was reminded of how strong women sometimes have to be. A man had died in Thailand, leaving behind his wife who was five months pregnant. The couple must have been full of excitement and anticipation over their child, whom they had tried for without success until they resorted to in vitro fertilization, or IVF.

Just before he died, her husband had heart surgery, but had to travel to Thailand for work, where he died of congestive heart failure. This was the first time I attended to the funeral of someone who was leaving behind his pregnant wife. The woman was distraught—her husband had been her teenage sweetheart, and I understood from another family member that she wanted to kill herself. I do not know how she pulled herself through the darkness, but when I caught up with her later after her child was born, she had come to terms with her husband's passing and was channeling all her energy to her offspring.

CHAPTER 10

Red String and Incense

*T*raditional Chinese funerals, like traditional Chinese weddings, are becoming rare in modern and increasingly secular Singapore.

But when I was a child in the early eighties, I witnessed the pageantry and grandeur of a traditional Chinese funeral. My paternal grandmother, paternal grandfather, and maternal great-grandfather were all sent off in style, complete with grand processions, bands, and loud mourning.

Historically, Chinese death rituals in Singapore are complex with layers of meaning and interpretation, and differ with each dialect group. The forefathers of the Chinese in Singapore were immigrants who streamed in from different regions of China. The main dialect groups in Singapore, in descending order of the sizes of their populations, are: Hokkien, Teochew, Cantonese, Hakka, Hainanese, Foochow, Henghua, Shanghainese, and Hockchia.

There are also different religious considerations if the families of the dead are Buddhist or Taoist. The Taoists have death rites that are far more complex than those of the Buddhists. A stickler for tradition would have to consider both the dialect and religious aspects. A Cantonese Taoist funeral ritual might involve a priest, dressed in long robes and a special headpiece, jumping over a small fire to symbolically represent breaking through the ramparts of Hell; while a feature of a Hainanese Taoist funeral is colorful sand sculptures spread on the ground in various shapes, such as a dragon, embedded with flags and coins. A Teochew style funeral has a *shan tang* (善堂), where a group of Teochew singers sing a tune to remind us of filial piety, and the crossing of a bridge, which represents the journey of the deceased.

In a modern society, these rituals are fast losing relevance. Chinese who are atheists or freethinkers do not abide by them, although there are those who, despite embracing other faiths, still look over their shoulder to observe some traditions just in case there might be some truth behind the superstitions. Amongst the funerals that I organize, about 10 percent or less adhere to the full traditional requirements.

Moreover, families in Singapore are becoming increasingly diverse as people marry outside of the race and religion they were born into. In 2015, interethnic marriages comprised 21.5 percent of all marriages, up from 14.9 percent in 2005.

This can potentially lead to conflict at funerals, which I have witnessed first-hand. Several years ago, I attended to the funeral of a Chinese Taoist man whose son had become a Christian and whose daughter had converted to Islam after she married a Malay-Muslim. When we brought his body to the void deck where his wake was to be held, his wife started crying loudly in Hokkien. She was upset that their children had refused to kneel down and offer joss sticks, in the Taoist tradition, to show their respect and devotion to their father. Their son had also refused to carry a special flag on his shoulder that symbolized the soul of the deceased. She bemoaned that the same fate would befall her when she died. Finally, it was the deceased's Muslim son-in-law who held the joss sticks and carried the flag. Upon seeing him do so, his wife, the deceased's daughter, relented and held the joss sticks.

Sometimes, diversity in religion results in multiple rituals. When my maternal great-grandmother died, she was feted with Buddhist, Taoist, and Christian funeral rites. As she herself was Taoist, the Taoist monk came to chant some prayers and burn paper items, and later a Christian service was held by a pastor as one of her children is a Christian. A Buddhist monk was also in attendance to chant prayers.

My professional focus has been to make family members aware that there is an option to commemorate the life of the deceased and have a more meaningful and memorable funeral, rather than dwelling on these rituals.

And yet, even as they are becoming less common, these rituals are important. I fully respect them and their significance to an older generation of Chinese Singaporeans.

Some people still adhere to these rituals, even if they themselves don't believe in them, because they are trying to be filial, or because their parents may have wanted traditional funerals. Filial piety is an integral part of Chinese culture.

Essentially, death in traditional Chinese culture is not perceived as an end in itself. There is a continued relationship between the living and the dead, and ancestors are believed to be protecting the family even from beyond the grave. That is why many Chinese families keep ancestral tablets in their homes. What has largely emerged, amongst the Chinese who do want to observe these funeral rituals, is a pared-down, uniquely hybrid Chinese Singaporean funeral that retains elements from here and there.

I do not claim an academic knowledge of traditional death rites, and others in the funeral trade might well disagree with what I have talked about in this chapter. These are but some of my observations that are distilled from my experience on how traditional Chinese funerals were carried out in the olden days and how practices have evolved.

If people are unfamiliar with the rites—which is almost always the case—we advise them. They then decide on how closely they want to follow it.

If You Are a Family Member

Do Not Hold Weddings Within Three Years of a Funeral

If the deceased has the same surname as you do—for example, if the person is your paternal grandfather—and you were preparing to get married, you either have to hold the wedding within 100 days of the funeral, or wait till three years have passed. But if it is your maternal grandfather who has died, you can continue with the wedding, as you don't share the same surname.

Add Years to the Age of the Deceased

Longevity is considered a blessing in Chinese culture. It is for this reason that the Chinese are considered as being a year old on their day of birth. Someone who is biologically 40 years old is thus 41 according to the Chinese lunar calendar. At funerals, some families still add years to the age of their loved one. The number of years added depends on the dialect group of the family, but the general rule is three years.

Sometimes, when the deceased is above 80 at the time of death, the family may feel it is not necessary to inflate the deceased's age as they have already lived to a ripe old age.

Be Present at the Deathbed

The scene, which is still often enacted in Chinese drama serials, is of the family patriarch or matriarch dying on a bed surrounded by children and grandchildren. Any descendant who did not make it back in time for the death used to be considered unfilial. But these days, family members often live in several different countries, and children who are working abroad might not be able to fly back in time, though most usually try to rush back when their parents are gravely ill.

Only sons, their wives, unmarried daughters, and grandchildren are required to make up the deathbed circle. Daughters who have married out of the family—and who may have taken on their husband's surname—are not required to be there, for they are no longer considered part of the same clan. However, in reality, they are usually present because their own parent is dying.

Do Not Touch Your Mother's Body After She Has Died

Instead, you have to first invite her older brother to assess her body to make sure that she has not been physically harmed. This stems from the belief that, while the woman belongs to another family when she marries out, she returns home to her clan once she dies and she has to be "returned" in good condition.

This may sound like an antiquated notion, but people in Taiwan and a handful of people in Singapore—mostly Taoists—still practice this. However, this has become more of a formality. Rather than examining her, the brother would most likely stand next to his sister and pronounce to the rest of the family, who would be kneeling on the floor with their heads bowed, that the funeral may proceed.

The Wake Must Last an Odd Number of Days

This would usually be three, five, or seven days from the day the person passed away. The Chinese have a saying, 好事成双, *hao shi cheng shuang*, which means "good things come in pairs." A funeral wake is inauspicious and thus must last an odd number of days. The duration of the wake depends on how many visitors the family thinks there will be. In practical terms, expenses are a factor to consider, as each additional day adds to the costs of the funeral.

The Wake Must Be Set Up in the Day
The Chinese believe that life is a balance between yin and yang, two halves of a circle that flow into each other. The white half is yang, which denotes elements that are positive, bright, and masculine. The black half is yin, which denotes negativity, darkness, and the feminine. Night is associated with the dark forces, when spirits roam.

In instances where my staff have completed the setup at the wake venue, but the body is only ready after 7 pm when night has fallen, I check with the family if they would prefer to delay sending the deceased home until the next morning.

Place an Oil Lamp With a White Piece of Cloth Attached to it at the Entrance to the Wake
The light, with the white cloth that symbolizes death, is meant to guide the wandering spirit of the deceased back home. A more logical explanation may be that in the olden days, when people in Singapore lived in *kampongs*, or villages, that did not have streetlights and proper roads, the oil lamp simply served as a location marker and guided visitors to where the wake was being held.

Place Red Paper or Ribbons where Appropriate to Protect Others from Bad Luck
Red is the color of luck, and it protects against evil, darkness, and death. For that reason, funeral directors paste red squares of paper where appropriate during a funeral to protect the neighbors from bad luck.

For instance, if a funeral was being held at the void deck of a block of flats and the deceased stayed on the sixth floor of that block, we paste red squares at the lift landings and staircases of the first and sixth floors so neighbors can safely return home without being tainted by death. In the past, before lifts were built to serve every floor, we pasted these squares at every level near the staircase that the deceased would have passed by on his way home. Also, if one has to walk past other flats after emerging from the lift on the sixth floor before reaching the home of the deceased, we will paste the squares outside all of these neighbors' flats.

If the wake was held at a house, we attach small red satin ribbons on the gates of the neighbors living around that house. We approach the neighbors and explain what we are doing. If they don't believe in superstition and would rather not have us attach the ribbon, we will respect their wishes.

We also tie red ribbons around the abdomens of pregnant family members who are present at the wake or funeral, although pregnant women are generally discouraged from attending them.

Cover all Mirrors, Idols, and Deities

If the wake was being held at the home of the deceased, or at the void deck of the deceased's HDB flat home, then all mirrors in the household or vicinity should be covered. This is to prevent death from being reflected and another death from occurring. Figurines and statues of deities like Guan Yin or the Kitchen God[9] have to be covered with red cloth or paper, for exposing the deities to death is inauspicious.

Wear a White Shirt and Dark Trousers

This is standard attire for immediate family members at most Chinese funerals. Extended family members and visitors should avoid wearing bright colors, such as red, yellow, and gold, because these are colors usually associated with happiness.

---

9 Guan Yin, the goddess of mercy, is often considered the most widely beloved Buddhist deity. She is an all-knowing and compassionate god whose name translates literally to "one who hears the world's cries."

Jewelry should not be worn. Some families, who are stricter about their funeral rituals, require the close family members of the deceased to be clad in coarse brown overcoats and headgear made of sackcloth. Tradition also dictates what they should wear under the sackcloth. The sons, eldest grandson, daughters, and daughters-in-law of the deceased should wear white button-down shirts. The sons-in-law should be dressed in dark mourning colors, but are not required to wear the sackcloth. The siblings of the deceased should wear black; the daughters' children should wear blue; and the great-grandchildren should wear green.

Pin a Fabric Square on the Shirtsleeves of the Family Members

Small square pieces of colored cloth that measure about 3.5 cm on each side are attached with safety pins to the sleeves of family members on the first day of the wake. Called 孝, *xiao* (meaning "filial piety"), these bits of cloth are pinned on the left sleeve if the deceased is a man, and on the right sleeve for a woman. Its color depends on your relationship to the deceased, and different dialect groups have different color codes.

In China, these are worn for up to three years. In Singapore, people used to do the same, but the duration of the wearing of the xiao has decreased over the years. These days, family members dispense with the cloth after the funeral.

Dress the Body Appropriately

In the past, elderly Chinese who died were clad in a special outfit called 寿衣, *shou yi* (longevity clothing), that they would have bought for themselves while they were still alive. Outwardly, it is a traditional set of formal Chinese clothes—shiny satin, frog buttons, and sleeves—and includes a hat for the men, and a hairband with a pearl or jade jewel in the center for the women.

The number of layers of the funeral outfit, just like the number of days of a wake, must be an odd number—three, five, or seven—and there are more layers on the top of the body than below. If it is the father who has died, his son and daughter should dress his body. If it is the mother who has died, her body should be dressed by her daughter and daughter-in-law.

The shou yi is worn to keep the deceased warm on the "other side." The layers also pad up the body to give the impression that the deceased is fleshier than they really are, which connotes prosperity. The soul of the deceased can stride confidently into the afterlife as a well-fed tycoon, and not as a skinny pauper. Some believe that each layer represents a generation of descendants; the more layers, the more descendants the deceased will have.

The layers may also have served the practical purpose of absorbing body fluids that seeped out as a result of decomposition when embalming had not yet become common practice.

Nowadays, however, it is extremely rare for families to opt for shou yi. The dead are usually dressed in their favorite outfits, or formal attire.

Welcome the Deceased Home

This ritual relates mainly to Taoist funerals. As we bring in the body, which is placed on a stretcher, a red banner is strung up over the entrance to the wake venue. The deceased's children are to stand to the side and welcome him home. This practice of standing to the side usually applies to Teochew funerals.

Once the coffin is positioned at the wake venue, family members have to symbolically clean the deceased. We have already done the physical cleaning of the deceased, but families feel that it is important for them to take part in the purification process, for the belief is that an unclean person would be despised and punished in Hell.

We ask for permission from Tu Di Gong, the god of the soil and the ground, before we turn on the tap. While burning joss sticks and giving offerings, we tell Tu Di Gong that the water is meant to wipe the deceased's face, and throw a coin to see if permission is granted. Once the water is collected, family members stand in a specific order, based on their rank in the family. The eldest son or grandson of the deceased will wipe his face three times with a damp towel while uttering certain phrases. This is a symbolic gesture and the towel might not even touch the face.

After the cleaning, family members will symbolically feed the deceased. Each one in the line will press a few grains from a bowl of rice to the lips of the deceased with a pair of chopsticks.

Once this is complete, the body is shifted from the stretcher to the casket. This is when family members are expected to whisper words of farewell to the deceased.

Place a Pearl In the Mouth and Personal Belongings in the Casket

We place a pearl, of about 1 to 1.5 cm in diameter, into the mouth of the deceased. It is believed that the pearl will protect the deceased and can be used to "bribe" the judges in Hell. It also ensures that he will enjoy a smooth journey into the afterlife and be reincarnated into a good house. This is usually a Taoist ritual, but occasionally Buddhist families will also request it. Sometimes, we use a coin in place of a pearl.

We also place a bag of rice on top of the casket that will later be distributed to the various family members before the cremation, for it is believed that the rice has been blessed by the deceased. However, this practice has been simplified with time.

Other items that may be put into the casket and cremated along with the body include large amounts of paper money— for spending in the afterlife—and personal articles that usually include wallets, clothes, bags, and even shoes.

Nail the Casket Shut

Once we put on the lid of the casket, we hammer in the nails with an axe. It is symbolic: hammering in the nails to four corners of the casket, which symbolically represent north, south, east, and west. Then a nail will be hammered into the top middle edge of the coffin. Auspicious phrases must be said during this process.

The crucial nail is the one in the top middle edge of the coffin, known as a *zi sun ding*, 子孙钉 (son-grandchildren nail). We will eventually remove this nail before the cremation or burial, enclose it in a red packet, and give it to the deceased's eldest grandson. This ensures that he will have sons and that the family line will continue.

Offer Food on the Altar

This is a practice that is familiar to most Buddhists and Taoists even now, as many people still have prayer altars in their homes on which they burn joss sticks and place food as offerings to the gods and their ancestors.

At the wake, food is placed on the altar that has been set up for the wake. Resting on this altar is usually the photo of the deceased, as well as a joss pot for the joss sticks. The standard repertoire is a bowl of rice and an array of meat or vegetable dishes. Buddhists usually stick to vegetarian fare.

Mourn Visibly

Family members should observe the rules of grieving etiquette. This includes depriving oneself of pleasurable activities, including going out with friends, watching television, and indulging in good food. In the past, this period of mourning lasted one year. This was shortened to 100 days, and now to 49 days.

A public display of grief, usually through loud wailing, shows that the deceased was loved and is an expression of filial piety. When my paternal grandmother died, I remember being rather traumatized when I saw all my uncles and aunts in a frenzied state of grief as they surrounded her casket. But in a way, this ritual is emotionally cathartic.

In the past, there used to be professional mourners in Singapore—a group of about 10 to 12 elderly ladies—but this profession is dying out. In some places, such as Taiwan, paying for a professional mourner is still a common practice. Such mourners even throw themselves on the ground in front of the casket, or try to grab it as it is being taken away, as part of their fervent expressions of grief.

Keep All-Night Vigils

Family members take turns staying up all night at the wake to accompany the deceased, keep the incense lit throughout the night in the case of Buddhist and Taoist funerals, and fend off stray animals. It is considered bad luck if an animal were to jump over the casket. In the past, family members and friends who kept vigil would play mahjong to stay awake. The provision of Wi-Fi these days is critical, so family members can stay connected throughout the night.

Because families are getting smaller, it may be very tiring for the one or two children of the deceased to have to stay up every night during the duration of the wake, on top of having to attend to visitors in the day, all the while grappling with grief and after-death administrative matters. I thus get my staff to work the graveyard shift.

Hire a Band

Entertainment is provided during a Chinese funeral, especially during the final procession, to frighten away malicious spirits. It also entertains the guests, and shows that the deceased's offspring are filial and will splash out on the funeral. Some prefer Chinese oldies or contemporary music played by live bands. Others prefer more traditional types of entertainment, with Chinese gongs and drums accompanying big-headed dancing dolls. The shows were more elaborate in the past, with acts like stilt walkers. In places like Taiwan and China—but not in Singapore—there are even funeral strippers. They stand on a brightly lit electric flower car (similar to parade floats) that are part of the funeral procession, while dancing or gyrating around a pole, removing one piece of clothing after another to the consternation or delight of the audience as they are driven past.

Walk Behind the Casket

When it is time for the casket to leave for the crematorium, the casket is carefully loaded onto a hearse, which is then driven very slowly for a few hundred meters. The family and those who are attending the funeral walk behind the vehicle as they escort their loved ones on their final journey.

Burn Items for the Deceased's Use in the Afterlife

Those who are deceased continue living in Heaven (or Hell) after death. For them to enjoy a comfortable afterlife, their descendants are to "send" over all manner of creature comforts by burning the semblance of these items in miniature paper form. The burning usually takes place the night before the funeral. These could include elaborate multi-storied paper houses, luxury cars with chauffeurs, boats, private airplanes, even mobile phones and mahjong tables—all crafted from paper. The burning of paper money and goods continues during the annual Qing Ming Festival, or Tomb-Sweeping Day, a designated occasion for the Chinese to pay respects to their ancestors, and during the Hungry Ghost Festival.

If You Are a Visitor

Pregnant Women and Babies Should Stay Away

As death is considered inauspicious, pregnant women and children below the age of four are discouraged from attending wakes.

If a pregnant woman is there, however, she should not kneel when paying respects to the deceased, not only because it may be physically uncomfortable for her, but because her baby may be destined for a higher station in life than the deceased, and it would be unseemly for such a personage—albeit unborn—to be subservient before a lesser being.

Bring Money in a White Envelope

You should place some money in a white envelope to present at the reception, or personally gift it to the family. This *bai jin* (*"pek-kim"* in Hokkien), or white gold, is a cash contribution to help the bereaved family with their expenses. Individuals and corporations associated with the deceased might also send standing wreaths of flowers in muted colors, like white lilies, or banners. These appear as huge striped towels or blankets with condolence messages, which are strung up in a row.

Pay Your Respects

Upon arriving, you should light a single joss stick at the altar, usually in front of where the photograph is placed, and bow to the deceased while clasping the joss stick. Those who prefer not to burn the joss stick can bow in silence. A representative from the family will stand next to the altar table, facing you, and acknowledge the paying of respects with a bow.

Do Not Say Goodbye

When you leave, you should not say the Chinese word for "goodbye," 再见, *zài jiàn*, which is literally translated as "see you again" and is an inauspicious phrase to say at a wake, lest the next time you see the host is at another wake.

Throw Away the Red Thread After Leaving the Wake or Funeral

We place short lengths of thin red thread on the tables at the wake venue, which guests can take with them to ensure that they are protected from malicious spirits as they make their way home. Traditionally, the thread should be tied around the middle button of a man's shirt, somewhere near his chest. Alternatively, it can be tied around the finger. After you leave the wake or funeral, you can untie it and throw it away.

Wash With Flower Water

To cleanse yourself of bad luck, you should wash your hands in a tub of water that has loose flowers immersed in it once you reach home. We also provide this by placing some flower water at the funeral wake and at the crematoriums for use after the funeral service.

Chapter 11

Putting the "Fun" Back in "Funeral"

A funeral need not be a litany of rituals and book verses. It is an event that marks the end of a singular life—lying in the casket is not just a body, but a unique individual who was someone's child, sibling, parent, friend, colleague, boss, or mentor.

The first time I witnessed a personalized funeral officiated by a funeral celebrant was in Auckland, New Zealand. I had helped to embalm the person who was lying in the casket and the funeral director invited me to join in the funeral. The deceased had died at 94. She was petite, with a halo of permed snow-white hair, and she was wearing her spectacles in the casket as she had always worn them when she was alive. She wore her favorite pink lipstick which was provided by the family, and a matching pink scarf was slung around her neck. She seemed tremendously popular and well-loved, judging by the crowd that had gathered in the chapel. I was part of the embalming team.

At the start of the funeral service, the funeral director and funeral celebrant went up to the altar and bowed. The funeral director then made his way to the back of the chapel, leaving the funeral celebrant at the podium to speak about the lady. Other speakers followed, describing her, how she had made a difference to them and why she had been special. Up until then, I had never attended a funeral where I learned so much about the life of the deceased.

I discovered that she had been a notable volleyball coach and the many ladies in their seventies who were at the funeral had been her students, and had not forgotten her dedication. Her son joked that it was lucky he had been born a boy, for if he had been a girl, his mother would have made him join her volleyball squad.

Her eight-year-old grandson said, to the even greater amusement of those who were gathered there, "I love my Nana because she brought me to McDonald's without letting Daddy and Mummy know. She always made sure I got to soccer practice one hour early so that I could warm up."

The program sheets that had been given out to the guests did not just contain the order of service, but also a list of eulogists, photographs of the deceased, and her favorite poem. The funeral was an utterly charming event and if the old lady's spirit had been present, I'm sure she would have been delighted to hear what had been said.

People cried, laughed, and clapped. Layer by layer, like an onion being peeled, the years of her life were laid bare before me. I walked into the funeral of someone who was a stranger, but I left feeling as if she had been my friend. I felt I had known her for her whole life.

It was the experience of funerals like these that made me decide that I did not just want to be a funeral director—I did not just want to organize funerals; I wanted to celebrate lives, commemorate their legacies. A funeral celebrant officiates at a funeral with such a view, and I obtained my funeral celebrant certification in Australia in 2011. Such roles exist internationally and are known by different titles—in Australia and New Zealand, they are called Civil Funeral Celebrants; in the US and United Kingdom, they are known as Humanist Celebrants or Humanist Officiants. Such funerals, which celebrate life, are growing in popularity. In 2018, UK funeral provider Co-op Funeralcare surveyed 30,000 Britons and found that 41 percent of them desired such funerals.

Every aspect of such funerals reflects the personality and interests of the deceased.

Music, for one, is a crucial element. In New Zealand, I learned that there are specific names for about four pieces of music to be played at different key points in these funerals, just like how a wedding would feature processional music for when the bride is walking in, and recessional music for when the couple is walking out. At a funeral, this would include the Entry piece (for when the funeral visitors are arriving), the Eulogy piece (to accompany the reading of the eulogy), the Reflection piece (when visitors are asked to place flowers on the casket), and the Exit piece (when the visitors exit the hall). In Singapore, I also added a Viewing Hall piece because we have to move from the service hall to the viewing hall to observe the casket moving into the cremator. We make sure to provide audio equipment so that we can play music chosen by the family members of the deceased at any funeral venue. In Singapore, people tend to select wistful piano instrumental pieces or songs with meaningful lyrics.

In the case of the double suicide, where the wife had jumped to her death after her husband who had been suffering from depression, we managed to obtain the recording of a love song he had written while he was still a student in polytechnic. We played it at his funeral, his voice wafting through the funeral hall, singing, "Don't you know that I can't live without you?" accompanied by the strumming of his guitar. Even the photographer who had been hired to document the funeral shed a tear.

The food that is catered for the funeral can also be personalized. At a memorial service for a girl who was a Harry Potter fan, the guests at Hogwarts Burgers and Dumbledore Scallop Magnificent. At another memorial service, the food was catered by the favorite Indian restaurant of the man who had died. Teh tarik, his favorite drink, was included in the menu, and we made a toast to the deceased with the sweet tea. We set up a *muah chee* (Fujianese mochi) station at the memorial service of a lady who had loved the sticky local dessert.

Photo display boards have become very popular. We provide the decorative materials, and the families are given a large board that they fill up with photographs and captions. When we did a photo board for my father, one of the captions read: "Your favorite picture! It was a dream come true for you when Andy Lau, your idol, came to your shop for a local film production."

The act of combing through the family archives to select photos for the boards is therapeutic and emotionally cathartic. I have heard family members, while working on the boards, say, "Where was this photo taken? I didn't know Grandma was so pretty in her younger days! I never knew this happened!" This creates beautiful new memories and opens up channels of sharing and communication between those left behind, across generations, as they talk about what their loved ones had done in the past as well as discover new information about them.

As people increasingly live their lives online, those who die will leave behind enduring digital footprints. Memorial websites can be set up for friends and family to add photos, post memories, and upload videos for posterity. Some people even set up such websites for themselves while they are still alive.

A smell can bring on a flood of memories. Once, when I entered a lift, I suddenly had the very strong sensation that my late father had come home. The person who had taken the lift before I did probably used the same cologne my father had. During a funeral, a scent would be that much more powerful and evocative if family members smelled the aroma of the chocolate chip cookies Mum used to bake, or the bouquet of the exact same Ethiopian coffee that Dad used to drink.

The deceased's hobbies, passions, and likes could also be celebrated at his funeral. A man who loved to fold origami in his spare time, and who had taught his nieces and nephews how to fold them, had hundreds of origami creations made by the children scattered all over his casket. The girl who loved Harry Potter had books from the series and memorabilia from her personal collection displayed during her memorial service. Before the memorial service of an avid marathoner, a group of his former colleagues participated in a run they organized in his memory. A blanket with the Liverpool football club's logo and slogan "You'll never walk alone" printed on it was draped over a faithful fan's casket; family members and friends were invited to write well-wishes on the blanket, and the funeral pallbearers wore Liverpool jerseys.

We handled the funeral of a man who headed a team of divers at Underwater World Singapore (UWS), an aquarium that has since closed down. In what was believed to be the first such death in the country, he died after being stung by a stingray in October 2016. Mr. Philip Chan, who was in his early sixties, had been working at UWS for 25 years and was passionate about diving and the marine animals he worked with. For his funeral, we decked out the area with his diving gear, including his fins, air tank, weight belt, regulator, and diving boots. His diving suit was hung up and his mask was slung over the flower border of his photo. My staff also put up visuals of underwater scenes. The display would have struck a chord with his diving buddies and colleagues, who turned up in droves to say farewell to a man they clearly respected and loved.

On another occasion, in a deviation from the usually somber silence of the Mandai crematorium, we organized a funeral service there for a six-year-old special-needs boy that resounded with laughter from his Pathlight School classmates. They sang children's songs like "If You're Happy and You Know It." We screened a video montage that featured the little boy, with upbeat music as the soundtrack. His classmates snacked on sweets, lollipops, chips, and the deceased's favorite drink, Coca-Cola.

The South African parents of the child who had died after an operation were determined to celebrate his life at the funeral. They decided that his classmates should not see the boy in his casket. Instead, after a short service at the crematorium service hall, the guests adjourned to the reception area, while my staff witnessed the pushing of the casket into the cremator in a separate viewing hall.

Above all, it's the stories about the lives of the deceased that define these funerals—stories lovingly crafted from interviews conducted with families and friends. The funeral celebrant course in Australia taught me how to go about interviewing family members, structure and write funeral celebrant scripts, and handle sensitive cases of death—for example, where the deceased was a child, or had died from suicide. The sharing of such stories is rare during traditional Buddhist or Taoist funerals, but is becoming more common in Singapore.

Mr. Lim was my friend's father. I called him "Uncle"—he was, to me, a taxi driver whom I occasionally saw at Chinese New Year gatherings but whom I never spoke to. It was only when he died and my friend entrusted me to organize his funeral that I learned more about the person that he had been.

The family had managed to dredge up a photo of Uncle in his younger days, in which he sported an Elvis Presley hairstyle and posed next to a sports car. He had been the pampered eldest son of a wealthy couple who ran a successful restaurant in Chinatown. He used to drive sports cars, like the one he had taken a photo with, and liked to hang out and party with a group of friends.

When his father died, he was left in charge of the restaurant, but he had no idea how to run it. He had to close the restaurant and his fortunes went downhill. He became a taxi driver in order to support his family.

His children—including my friend—did not see much of him when they were growing up. I had a sense that he was ashamed of his fall from grace and was trying to get his feet back on the ground. In fact, with the help of his daughter, he managed to pass his taxi driving test despite not being able to speak a word of English. However, his three granddaughters had nothing but adoration for a man who, in his twilight years, had lavished his time and affection on them. He ferried his granddaughters around, brought them out and treated them to fast food.

I never knew any of his life history until he had died. It also became clear to me that we play many roles during our lifetimes, and different people at various points of our lives will know different sides of us. I hope that, as a life celebrant, I can help bring together all these sides of people for their families and friends to remember them by. And if you ever had the thought, "I don't want people to cry at my funeral," then a funeral with The Life Celebrant will suit you just fine.

CHAPTER 12

Showers of Love

When someone dies, it is perfectly okay to touch, kiss, and hold them as you would when they were alive. But people tend not to do that. What I observe is that after someone dies, most people seem to be afraid of touching the body. Do they think it is dirty or disrespectful?

I witnessed this fear when I recently attended to the funeral of an old lady.

I received the call from her grandson after dinnertime; he told me that she had died in her sleep. I rushed down to the family's residence immediately to assist them. When I entered the living room, about 20 family members were standing awkwardly outside the old lady's bedroom.

There was a police officer standing by the bedroom door. I asked the officer's permission to enter the room. The door was open and as I entered, I discovered her body lying on the floor instead of her bed, covered with a white sheet, with another police officer standing by the foot of her bed. I then asked permission from the officer to touch the old lady.

I found out that when she passed away in her sleep after her shower, the family had first called officers from the Singapore Civil Defence Force, who moved her to the floor and tried unsuccessfully to resuscitate her. When that failed, they called the police.

Without quite knowing what to do, and unsure of whether they could touch her, her family members left her body on the floor and covered her up with a white sheet—just like how it is sometimes done in drama serials!

When the police arrived, they told the family to call a doctor to certify the death of their mother/grandmother. The grandson called me immediately. I then called a doctor to head over to the residence to certify her death. (On a side note, when a natural death occurs, there is usually no need to call the police. The family just has to engage a funeral director, who can then arrange for a doctor to come over. It is only if the doctor is unable to ascertain the cause of death, that the police have to be summoned.)

When I got to the family residence, the doctor had not yet arrived. The family members must have found it surprising when I removed the sheet and started talking to her, introducing myself and telling her that I would be taking care of her. I took her pillow from her bed and placed it under her head, and covered her up with a blanket, folding it at her chest so it looked exactly like she was sleeping. Then I told the family members, "Your mum or grandma can still hear you. Do come in and speak to her."

They did, in Cantonese. I could tell from their faces that they were relieved when they saw that their beloved family matriarch looked more comfortable.

There is really no scientific or religious reason why we should not treat our loved ones the same way we did when they were alive. Perhaps preconceived notions—what others tell us or what we see from drama serials—teach us otherwise. But take it from me: Don't just treat your loved one as a corpse, to be feared once they pass on. Continue to shower your love on them.

That is one of the reasons we started Showers of Love, 留心语 *liu xin yu*, in 2017. It is a sanctuary where families can join us in the process of preparing their loved ones for their final journey. This is a process that is usually hidden; most times, bodies are taken away by the funeral director to be embalmed or dressed and prepared, and are returned, in the casket, to the wake venue. Families are oblivious as to how their loved ones are prepared for the funeral. Moreover, the lack of participation by the families may result in the deceased not having his or her usual hairstyle or makeup.

But at the Showers of Love sanctuary, which is attached to our office at the Geylang Bahru industrial estate, families can help us wash their loved one's face and hair, give a facial and dress the body, and help out with the makeup and hair styling. It is like a spa for the departed. With embalming that has been professionally done, it is a completely safe and hygienic process, carried out with guidance from my staff and me. The team comprises only women, and

I call them the Shower of Love Angels. The entire process is conducted in a respectful manner, without compromising the deceased's dignity.

The inspiration for Showers of Love actually struck me 12 years earlier, when I watched the Japanese movie *Departures*. The 2008 film, which became the first Japanese production to win an Academy Award for Best Foreign Language Film, stirred up worldwide interest in the beauty of funeral rituals and how the dead are sent off.

The film depicts a second-rate cellist who loses his job with an orchestra, stumbles into the funeral industry and finds his calling as a mortician, or *nokanshi*, a professional who prepares deceased bodies for their funerals. The film dwells at length on the encoffining, or *nokan*, ceremony. This formal Japanese ritual encompasses a skilled, almost dance-like, sanitizing of the dead body, the arrangement of its limbs, as well as the dressing up of and application of makeup on the body, while preserving the deceased's privacy and dignity.

The thought of introducing the concept of death care professionals involving family members in caring for their deceased loved ones simmered in my mind. I even visited Shanghai in 2015 when I heard that the Chinese had already introduced decedent care spas. But I was uncertain if there would be people in Singapore who would be open to it.

Then I got to know a wealthy Japanese family, who actually flew in four nokanshi from Japan to conduct the ceremony for the family patriarch. The nokanshi, who have to undergo one year of training before they can practice, flew in while the patriarch was still ill. They were put up at a hotel in Singapore for a week. When the elderly man eventually died, they conducted the small, private ceremony in the family's home, located in a condominium on Orchard Road. I was then even more determined to start Showers of Love.

In 2017, people were slow to take to the idea. Perhaps it was the first time they had come across such a service and needed time to get used to the concept. But gradually, it has become increasingly popular, and it was Showers of Love that helped us to win the Most Innovative Award at the Women Entrepreneur Awards in July 2019, on top of my being one of the Pulsar Category award winners.

The entire Showers of Love sanctuary comprises a lounge area where family members can rest and help themselves to drinks, snacks, and hot meals like macaroni and cheese, *hor fun*, and teriyaki chicken rice. Often, in the midst of planning a funeral, people forget about their hunger, and it is only when they are in a relatively relaxed atmosphere that hunger kicks in. We introduced the hot meals when we realized that people relished the snacks. The actual room itself has a raised dressing table in the center where they can observe the deceased being showered, made up, and dressed. The family members are free to participate in any part of the process.

Beyond the shower itself, some people are even choosing to use the Showers of Love sanctuary as a venue for visitation, which is more common in Western countries and is different from a wake, as the body is not in a casket. In the visitation, which lasts for a few hours, friends and family can come and say goodbye in a more intimate way, hugging the deceased or holding their hand in farewell.

A memorable visitation that was held at Showers of Love was for former S-League soccer player and coach, Darren Stewart, who was 52 when he died on October 18th, 2018. The Australian, who was named Australian Player of the Year in 1993, had lived in Singapore since 1999, when he signed on to play for Balestier Central. He later became a much-loved S-League coach.

Suffice it to say, there were many who wanted to bid him goodbye. We dressed him in his club's green soccer jersey so he looked exactly like he was going to play a game. The divorcee had a son and daughter, and when they saw him, they decided that he didn't need to be in a casket. Culturally, the Australians do not regard the casket as a must-have, and at the time, fortuitously, we were the only funeral provider in Singapore who could set up a visitation sans casket. Mr. Stewart was laid on the dressing table, where people could touch him if they wanted to. He wasn't covered with any blankets either, as his family wanted his whole jersey to be seen.

Even his dog, an adorable Maltese called Stef, hung out at our place. After his divorce, Mr. Stewart was left with the dog, which he did not like at first, but who later became his best friend. At Showers of Love, the dog lay silently on the bed right next to him throughout the visitation, seemingly in contemplation of the fact that her owner had passed away.

It was a cozy event, full of not just heartfelt tears, but laughter. As the funeral celebrant, I collected and shared many stories of Mr. Stewart, fondly known to his friends as Dazza. I was told that he did not use a watch to measure time; instead, he used cans of beer to estimate how long it took to reach a destination. The moment I said that, his father, who was in his seventies, popped open a beer, to chortles all around.

The photos of the funeral, at first glance, appear to be of a celebration as there were much smiles and laughter. But one of my favorite photos captured a poignant moment when Mr. Stewart's son hugged him farewell as he was laid on the dressing table.

Showers of Love has also been a boon to parents who want to send their deceased children off in a meaningful way. No other funeral company in Singapore allows parents to bathe their deceased children. When children die, the Chinese in particular have traditionally preferred the funeral to be over and done with quickly. But with Showers of Love, I think we tapped into a need.

One of the children who used our Showers of Love sanctuary, and whom I will always remember, was Misha Peh. She was a six-year-old girl who died of cancer in September 2018. She was diagnosed with diffuse intrinsic pontine glioma (DIPG), a malignant form of a brain tumor in children, when she was just four years old. The only child had a visitation which lasted three days at our sanctuary, which she herself had planned for before she died. She wanted to have a princess party, because she felt that "funerals are for the dead."

As she was laid on the dressing table, she was covered with flowers, toys, paper hearts, and origami cranes left by visitors. They could whisper farewell in her ear, and in return they each received a Thank You note she had written when she was alive. These notes featured a selected photo of hers, a verse from the Bible which said, "All go to the same place; All come from dust, and to dust all return. Ecclesiastes 3:20," and the words "Thank You! Love, Misha" handwritten in rainbow colors.

The Showers of Love sanctuary was decorated with items that she had pre-selected. She conveyed her wishes through her mother, who would instruct us via WhatsApp messages. Misha had chosen to deck her funeral space with rainbow-colored baby's breath flowers, and she had personally chosen all the colorful balloons, because she had made it clear that she wanted lots of glitter and rainbow colors at her funeral. She took weeks to create two photo collages for her funeral, handpicking each photograph and arranging them herself, and she even picked a dress as her final outfit from a selection we found for her from a children's clothes shop. It was white with glittering gold stars, complete with wings and a halo.

Subsequently, when she was brought to the Mandai Crematorium to be cremated, the hall where visitors gathered for her service was similarly decorated with balloons, baskets, and bouquets of flowers. As guests took their seats, an instrumental version of "I See the Light" from Disney's animated film *Tangled* played softly from the overhead speakers. She was dressed in the outfit she chose in her little white casket, decorated with a specially designed sticker she had chosen which said, "Little Angel Misha."

She was the first child I have met who, at a tender age, was able to calmly accept and plan for her own funeral. It must have been a strange experience for her mum to have had to "clear" and "approve" decorations and funeral arrangements with her dying daughter! I felt that she was an old soul in a child's body.

Her parents spoke to online magazine *Rice Media*, and what they said brought a tear to my eye. On her resilience, her mother, Rynthia Mathew, said, "For us to figure out if she's in pain, it's hard to tell because she'll control herself until it's really severe. Then, she'll ask you for medication. She'd rather control herself and see us smile, than to see us cry."

They also told me that whenever she had to have an injection and cried out of pain, she would apologize to her parents for crying. She did not want her beloved mum and dad to feel her pain.

Her father, Peh Wei Hao, described what Misha told him: "She told me to take care of my wife and to love my wife." As for her last words, Rynthia remembered her whispering, "I love you, Mommy. I love you, Daddy. I love you, Jesus."

Through tending to Misha and other children who are facing death, I had a revelation: not every child is afraid of death. Some are aware of it, face it bravely, and even try to remain strong for their heartbroken parents.

I asked the question to a friend of mine who had leukemia as a child: Weren't you ever afraid? He told me, "No, I never actually understood the intensity of what I myself was going through even though I could see that my parents were very sad. I was more concerned with the fact that they were sad, as well as my hair loss from chemotherapy treatments and having to miss school, than over the fact that I might die."

But for those who sadly pass away, what families can do at Showers of Love are simple acts of love for their child. Being able to say goodbye in a meaningful and emotional manner, where the dead are regarded not as bodies to be feared but as loved ones who are sleeping forever, gives a gratifying sense of closure and is emotionally cathartic.

We based this understanding on the Five Love Languages, a concept adopted from the book by Dr. Gary Chapman. It outlines how people express love in different ways, via words of affirmation, physical touch, gifts, quality time, and acts of service. Showers of Love grants families and visitors the opportunity to say farewell in all five love languages, so they can express their gratitude while being able to grieve and heal.

CHAPTER 13

The Journey Home

Y ou are blessed (or very young) if you have never had to call a funeral director.

Organizing a wake and holding a funeral is like planning a rather complicated event. And other than religious considerations, there are many things that family members will have to do when someone dies.

Certifying the Death

Singapore law requires that all deaths must be registered within 24 hours with the following documents: the certificate of the cause of death (issued by an authorized medical practitioner), the identity card and passport of the deceased (which have to be cancelled), as well as those of the person who is bringing these documents for registration. Only then will the death certificate be issued.

If the cause of the death is known and it occurred at a public or government-restructured hospital, the registration can be done there. If the death takes place at a private hospital or at home, the registration has to be done at any neighborhood police center, police post, or the police divisional headquarters. It can also be done at the Immigration and Checkpoints Authority.

If the cause of death is unknown or if foul play is suspected, the body of the deceased will be transferred to the Mortuary@ HSA, which is located at Block 9 of the Singapore General Hospital. While every hospital has a mortuary, this is the only forensic facility in Singapore where autopsies can be conducted.

The media sometimes gather outside the facility to take photographs of the family members of those who died under newsworthy circumstances. Usually, family members are asked to go there to identify the deceased, and this is also when they are told if their loved ones require an autopsy.

Transferring the Body

Once we get a call informing us that someone's loved one is dead, we need to transfer the body from the place of death to our Care Center. When we go down to the hospitals, the body is usually still lying in the ward, and is only moved when the funeral directors arrive and the families sign off to release the body to us through the mortuary.

Wake and Funeral Arrangements

Like an event management company, we have to work out the details of the wake and funeral with our clients, the deceased's family members.

Usually, this discussion is a harried affair, which sometimes takes place right in the corridors of the hospital where the patient has died. Funeral directors, on occasion, rush down when they are called, only to find that a competitor has snatched away their business. My mother and I once made a frantic dash to meet a potential client at 4 am, only to be told that he had decided to engage the services of someone else. The planning of such an important event should not be rushed. A hospital is also not the ideal place to talk about how to bid farewell to someone forever, especially if discussions are carried out late at night and the family members are physically and emotionally drained from a prolonged bedside vigil.

Before I set up the Showers of Love sanctuary, where visitors can rest comfortably and go through the funeral arrangements, I would tell the family members to go home and rest, and meet me in my showroom later or the next day, especially if it's already late at night. The showroom in my father's shop is a comfortable, air-conditioned space with displays of caskets and other collateral (such as urns) that the family can select from. They should also take time to choose the set of clothes that their loved one is to wear in the casket. If it is more convenient for the family, I can even meet them at home and they can choose a casket by viewing them from photos on my tablet.

Most people don't know that there is a difference between a casket and a coffin. A coffin has six sides, and a casket has four sides. We even have some with eight sides, for those who want their final resting place to have an auspicious number of sides, and eight is traditionally the most auspicious number for the Chinese. Christians tend to choose white caskets and, while the preference amongst Buddhists and Taoists is for caskets decorated with motifs like lotus flowers, we've started to observe more and more Buddhists choosing white caskets as well. In Singapore, the handles on caskets look as if they are made of metal, but they are actually decorative, flimsy, and made of plastic. That's why pallbearers grip the case by the bottom, never by the handles, which are not actually sturdy enough to hold up the casket. However, some caskets from overseas have handles that are weight-bearing.

When I saw that there were some people who wanted to personalize and customize a casket or coffin, I started bringing in models that could be fixed up in eight minutes. You could call it Make-Your-Own coffin. Made of wood, each of these can bear weights of up to 300 kg (660 lbs) and are popular with parents who want these for their deceased child. They can design, decorate, and write messages on the sides of these coffins.

For the funeral of a four-month-old baby, we customized her coffin by turning her photographs into stickers, which we pasted all over the coffin, collage-style, giving it a semblance of warmth. While making the wake and funeral arrangements, I have also learned that it is crucial to identify and engage with the person everyone else in the family looks to when decisions need to be made.

Decedent Care

At the Care Center, even for those who are not going to be embalmed, we at least bathe them and prepare the body for the wake. Not every funeral service director does this. I have seen instances where people who die at home are simply given a quick wipedown. I strongly disagree with this practice because everyone deserves a final bath and to be made to look presentable with their eyes and mouth closed, to leave beautiful lasting memories for those left behind. This is one of the reasons I started the Showers of Love sanctuary. There are rare instances, however, when family members do not want us to bring their loved ones back to the Care Center. I recently had a family that wanted us to do Showers of Love for their sister at her own home—just dressing her and putting her makeup on. She had passed away in hospice in the evening. In order to fulfill the wishes of the family, we sent her home around 11 pm after the embalming was done. My Showers of Love Angels helped ensure her makeup was according to how she used to wear it, and her hairdo, too. It gave a lot of comfort to the family to have her home before starting the funeral wake at the void deck the next day.

The Wake

It is believed that the term "wake" originated in England centuries ago, when people stayed up to keep watch over their loved one's body. Due to the lack of proper medical equipment to certify that a person was clinically dead, the fear was that the deceased might have been asleep or in a faint and wake up to find themselves trapped in a box. There were recorded instances in the late 19th century where graves were exhumed and the bodies were found with mutilated hands, with fingernail marks on the undersides of the coffin lids. Thus, family members stayed awake to make sure that the dead, if they woke up, were rescued and not prematurely buried.

With modern medical equipment and techniques that conclusively determine if a person has died, a wake has evolved to become an occasion when the family members and friends of the deceased are given an opportunity to pay their respects and say goodbye.

Once the body has been prepared and is placed in the casket, we send it to the venue of the wake. There are different venues in Singapore where you can hold wakes, such as void decks, churches, and funeral parlors. Most condominiums do not allow wakes, but if you live on landed property, you can hold it at your home. All you need is a permit from the Land Transport Authority if the wake will encroach onto the road outside your house. It is very common for wakes to be held at the void decks of HDB flats or multipurpose halls nearby, as over 80 percent of the population reside in these flats. This requires a permit from the town council.

In a rare instance when a family living in high-rise private property wanted to hold a wake at their home, my team brought up the casket in a lift. It was placed in the middle of the huge living room of their apartment that overlooked Orchard Road, Singapore's main shopping street. The deceased was a prominent personality, but rather than organize a large-scale wake that is normally the case for such VIP deaths, the family opted for a private, low-key funeral at home, which was attended by fewer than 10 people.

In the case of an Indian gentleman who lived in a swanky condominium at Bukit Timah, his wake was held at home because his family member was in the management committee of the condominium he lived in. Approval was easily obtained. His casket was placed in the large living room against the backdrop of a large painting that dominated the space. We simply rearranged the furniture, so visitors really felt as if they were just visiting the family. Hundreds of origami cranes hung from the ceiling, in line with the Japanese theme of the decor.

Once, we even had a swimming pool boarded up to create a platform for guests to sit on at the private residence.

Increasingly, people have been renting spaces that are designated wake venues as it is more convenient. These funeral parlors, the locations of which are designated by the government, may be found on industrial estates or in areas that don't cause a disruption to people living nearby.

To meet growing demand for wake venues that are accessible, the Singaporean government is launching four new funeral parlor sites to be developed over the next 10 years or so. These will be at Ang Mo Kio, Bukit Batok, Woodlands, and Mandai.

But there are those who will still find these sites inaccessible, and prefer the wake venue to be at the void deck of their HDB flat. They also want comfort. Thus, we have been turning void decks into air-conditioned "parlors" by enclosing the space with a tentage canvas, and bringing in air conditioning units. With soft white cloths forming contour scallops on the ceiling, and tables and chairs draped in white, the whole setup is elegant and refined.

It is the funeral director's job to take care of the rental of such a venue and to organize the entire event, including setting up the tents, altar, hospitality area for drinks and coffee, and a mobile toilet (if the wake is being held at a void deck). We prepare the site according to the family's religious wishes and beliefs.

Not everyone has to have a wake. Wakes are not usually organized when babies die. For those who die at a relatively young age or were single when they died, the tradition is for a brief funeral followed immediately by the cremation. Also, when the death is traumatic, the cremation may sometimes be held immediately.

However, more people are bucking this tradition, and my Angel Star service—personalized funerals for children—meets their needs.

The Funeral

The funeral is when the family and friends of the deceased are given the opportunity to say their last farewells before the deceased is buried or cremated. What happens during a funeral varies across religions. A pastor will conduct the service for a Christian funeral, while monks clad in saffron robes will chant prayers for a Buddhist funeral. For Catholics, the body has to be brought to church for Mass before departing to a crematorium or cemetery.

The funeral hearse is a vehicle that transports the casket to the burial ground or the crematorium, and bears a photo of the deceased at its front. There are a variety of hearses that are used during funerals in Singapore. The hearses in the past were extremely colorful, embellished with bright, shiny accessories and flashing lights, with the funeral portrait placed high at the top of the lorry hearse; some of these are still used.

In the seventies, my father started using a hearse that was a modified van with large windows through which passers-by could see the casket as the vehicle passed through the streets. Sometimes, lorries were also used. In recent years, there has been the option of limousine-style hearses that offer more privacy. Some car brands also set aside cars specifically to function as funeral hearses, including Ferrari, Lamborghini, and Tesla. We even brought in a Toyota Prius hybrid hearse.

Burial

Due to the lack of land in Singapore, people hardly opt to bury their deceased loved ones unless their religion requires them to do so, such as Islam.

Graveyards have been progressively exhumed over the years to make space for the living, one of the most high-profile being the plot of land where the Ngee Ann City shopping mall now stands. The Tai Shan Ting cemetery was formerly bounded by Paterson Road, Orchard Road, and Grange Road. There was even a temple that stood on its grounds. In September 1951, a ceremony was held before the mass exhumation of the remains of those who had been buried in that cemetery; $500 million in gold and silver "hell money" was burned to appease the dead. A Buddhist priest conducted the ceremony, while officials paid their respects and apologized to those whose remains had to be exhumed. The latest graveyard that had to be exhumed in Singapore, starting from 2013, was the Bukit Brown Cemetery. It will make way for a new four-lane road and a housing estate.

The Choa Chu Kang Cemetery Complex is the only cemetery in Singapore that still accepts burials. Thousands of tombstones are tightly packed next to one another there. Those who are buried there can only remain so for 15 years, after which the plot will be recycled. This was a policy introduced by the government in November 1998 to address the shortage of land in Singapore.

These burial plots are also not freshly dug, the way they would have been in the past. Instead, since 2007, the dead have been buried in concrete boxes that have already been set into the ground, just 15 centimeters apart, a utilitarian and pragmatic solution to meet burial needs in a land-scarce country. After the 15-year "lease" expires, the remains may be cremated and, if they remain unclaimed by the next of kin for three years, will be scattered at sea. If the deceased's religion does not permit cremation, the remains may be reburied into smaller individual plots. In these new plots, the remains of eight to 16 people may be packed into one space.

Cremation

Cremations are held at the Mandai Crematorium and Columbarium Complex, which is managed by the government, or at two private crematoriums: the Kong Meng San Phor Kark See Monastery at Bright Hill Drive, or the Tse Toh Aum Temple at Sin Ming Drive.

The furnace burns at an intense 700 to 900 degrees Celsius to dry the body, burn the skin and hair, contract and char the muscle, vaporize the soft tissue, and calcify the bones. On average, it takes one to three hours to cremate a human body, reducing it to about 2 kg to 3 kg (4.5 to 6.5 lbs) of remains, depending on the size of the body.

In Singapore, bodies are still cremated in caskets. In the United States, cremation surpassed traditional burial rates for the first time in 2015, at 49 percent nationwide, compared to 10 percent in 1980. This could be because cremation can be thousands of dollars cheaper than burial because of the cost of a burial plot. An increasingly popular option in the US is for bodies to be placed in special cardboard boxes, which are inserted into rented caskets for the wake but are then taken out for the cremation. It is not only cost-effective but also environmentally friendly, as the boxes burn more easily.

Sorting Out the Cremains

After the body is cremated, what is left behind is light grey ash and white bone fragments. It takes about 30 minutes to an hour for it to cool. The crematorium staff will then remove anything that is not bone, like wood or nails, which were part of the casket. The rubble may also include metal tooth fillings, surgical screws, and implants. In some overseas crematoriums, magnetic devices are used to make a "sweep" over the burnt material to extract metallic fragments.

Practices vary across crematoriums, but at the Mandai Crematorium, the staff will then place the bone fragments into an incongruous plastic storage box with a lid. This box is reused, which has caused discomfort to the members of some families, and is a practice I hope will change in the future. In Toronto, Canada, I saw how cremains were ground and individually packed into biodegradable bags, properly sealed, and labelled with serial numbers.

Family members are then invited into a private room to select pieces from the plastic box. Staff from the funeral company or the specialist from the columbarium are on hand to help out. We first seek out the skull, which, although broken, is usually the largest, smoothest piece. Then we look for other large bone fragments, like the femur (thigh bone), which is the longest bone in the human body. The bone fragments can further be ground into a coarse powder. It is a service that crematoriums provide, and is particularly helpful if the cremains need to fit into a small container like an urn. In Singapore, if the cremation takes place before noon, the cremains can be collected after 2 pm. If the cremation takes place after noontime, family members can collect it the next day. Sometimes, I have families that have not decided on the final resting place. As such, we will transfer the cremated remains of the departed into our care first, and once the family makes a decision, we will then transfer the cremated remains to the columbarium. It is very crucial for the family to decide on the final resting place of the departed carefully if the departed did not leave any instructions or pre-book a columbarium niche. The final resting place is like buying a property—you want to find a comfortable home in the afterlife, so families should never rush into this decision.

Memorial

Other than placing the cremains in a columbarium niche, these days there are many options for people to memorialize their loved one's remains in unusual ways. In some other countries, cremains are blended into concrete and used to make environmentally safe reefs (an idea that originated in Florida). Some have also divided the cremains and placed them in teddy bears for various family members as keepsakes.

What people do in Singapore is relatively sedate. Some choose to place the cremains in an urn, which is then tucked into grid-like niches at a columbarium. Some families have pre-booked several niches next to each other so that their cremains can be placed side by side with those of other family members.

Another increasingly popular option amongst Buddhists and Hindus is to scatter cremains into the sea. Christians are also more open to sea burials as it is not part of their faith to revere the dead, whom they believe have returned home to be with God.

A few family members can hire a bumboat, which will travel out to the ocean. At a designated point, a monk or priest will perform the last rites. Once the family members have said their farewells, the cremains are released into the water. In Singapore, cremains can be scattered in the waters off Changi, or at a designated site about 2.8 km (1.7 miles) south of Pulau Semakau, off southern Singapore.

I personally believe, however, that it is important to have a physical reminder of the departed in some form. I have often had elderly people tell me that they wish to have their cremains scattered into the sea because they do not wish to be a burden to their children in the future. They do not want their offspring to have to spend money on a niche or go through the duty of visiting the columbariums or cemeteries during the Qing Ming Festival—a sentiment that I actually find very sad. For centuries, memorial sites have played an important role in allowing people to go somewhere to remember their loved ones, and scattering cremains at sea is an irreversible act.

From 2020, the Singapore government has permitted inland ash scattering, whereby ashes can also be scattered on land. This has been available at Choa Chu Kang Cemetery Complex since 2020 and Mandai Crematorium and Columbarium Complex since 2021. According to *The Straits Times*, the ashes could be scattered in a garden within the facilities.

Turning cremains into diamonds is also becoming more commonplace. About 500 g (1.1 lbs) of ash will result in a diamond that can be mounted on a ring or strung on a necklace so, if you like, you can have your loved one next to your heart, or around your finger, forever.

In 2017, I introduced the idea of bio-urns, where cremains are placed in a pot together with soil to nurture a plant. People liked the notion of life arising from death, and as these plants can be placed at home, it means that they can keep their loved ones with them. When we first brought in these bio-urns from Spain, we had to adapt them because the original plants—like maple, oak, pine, redwood, and honey locust—would not survive in Singapore. They would also grow into trees, which may not be feasible here.

After consulting three horticulturalists, we changed the seeds to varieties of sturdy plants which can be kept at home without requiring much care. These include the Zeezee plant, Japanese pine, fiddle-leaf fig tree, and desert rose.

It is interesting to note that one person's cremains are sufficient to be split into different parts, which can be kept by different members of the family. For instance, in the case of 11-year-old Neal Chia's funeral, his cremains were split into five portions. The biggest portion was used in a bio-urn. Two portions were used to make necklaces which were given to his mother and uncle, while another two were placed in specially designed golf-themed containers; his father then decided to scatter the cremated remains in two golf courses in Indonesia, where the boy had played and scored two holes-in-one.

We offer biodegradable land urns; this is recommended for families that prefer to bury the cremated remains in their freehold land. Over time, the urn will disintegrate into the soil, hence ashes to ashes, dust to dust.

We also have biodegradable sea urns, which is a much more dignified way of scattering cremated remains into the ocean. Rather than tossing the bones and ashes directly into the sea or tying them up in a cloth bag, the bowl-shaped urn with a lotus or dolphin design, crafted by hand from recycled and kraft paper, is used instead. It is engineered to float briefly before sinking. Once submerged, these urns will break down naturally over time.

CHAPTER 14

Death Around the World

When they travel, most Singaporeans focus on food, shopping, or scenery. I, on the other hand, head for the nearest funeral home or cemetery, and sometimes even make arrangements to be attached to funeral service companies to observe the operations for a day or two. Or I offer my services to the funeral companies and be their extra pair of hands for a couple of days, so that I can immerse myself in their funeral culture.

The death rites of other countries—especially those that contrast with what is done in Singapore—fascinate and inspire me. To me, these rites are as illuminating about a country's culture as participating in a national festival or event, for the manner in which we say farewell to the dead says a lot about a country and its people.

Some countries have out-of-this-world practices. In Taiwan, professional mourners are sometimes hired for funerals, as are strippers; the latter is also practiced in China. Puerto Rico has a tradition where the deceased is embalmed to look lifelike for viewing, such as David Morales, who could be seen at his own funeral astride a motorcycle; or Fernando Diaz Beato, who was sat in a chair with his eyes open. This hit the headlines because it was the first case of extreme embalming featuring open eyes.

A video that went viral and had tongues wagging around the world was the Ghana Coffin Dance. These pallbearers dance with the coffin to celebrate the deceased person's life. They became known as "coronavirus grim" and even have a tongue-in-cheek Covid-19 message: "Stay home or dance with us."

Japan

In Japan, death is revered with what I would describe as a quiet, stoic dignity.

The emphasis on respect and orderliness is a hallmark of Japanese culture. When one steps into a Japanese funeral facility, the first impression one has is how clean and neat everything is; this, I suppose, is the general impression one gets of most things in Japan. In the embalming room I visited, waste material was very responsibly filtered and cleaned in-house before it was flushed away into the sewage system.

The needs of every visitor were anticipated and met. The parlor has an in-house florist so that visitors do not have to order them from elsewhere, which is usually the case in Singapore. This is to allow the parlor to be set up with the same floral wreath arrangement. While there was the usual condolence counter—with a guest book, pens, and envelopes for visitors to write messages to the family—a thoughtful touch was the provision of various strengths of reading glasses for long-sighted older folk who may have forgotten to bring their own. When visitors left, they were sometimes given a bag with souvenirs such as incense and towels.

The parlor had a family room, as luxurious as a good hotel room, in which family members could rest and even stay overnight. Some parlors even have bathtubs. According to the funeral homeowner, he says that it is their culture for families to share a bath together. The bedroom was large, clean, and well equipped with tatami-style beds; had a separate living room with a plush couch and a flat-screen television; and had neatly folded white laundered towels in the bathrooms.

As I walked through the parlor, the funeral staff stopped in their tracks, bowed, and greeted me, even if they were in the middle of a task. I noticed that there was a mirror inside the staff office, next to the door. The staff checked their appearances and made sure they looked presentable before they stepped out.

One of the most impressive funerals I witnessed in Japan was that of an old lady who used to coach geishas in their art. She must have been a geisha herself. The huge funeral hall was decorated to pay homage to what she had done in her life. There was a sophisticated display of handicrafts, handmade fans, umbrellas, and a television that screened videos of her dancing. In the center of it all was a photograph of the lady herself; it was not just a headshot, but a full-body photograph of her clad in her kimono. Her casket was placed discreetly between a table used for offerings and an elaborate multi-tiered altar decorated with flowers.

In Japan, death is but a part of life's journey. One of the largest funeral companies in Japan, the Sun-Life Corporation, also runs childcare facilities and homes for the elderly. It takes care of life, from birth to death.

I visited Japan in April 2019, where I was struck by how they had come up with the idea of mobile care facilities. This was an extension of the traditional *nokan* ceremony, where the body is ritually prepared, dressed, and made presentable, and which inspired our Showers of Love sanctuary. In Japan, it can now all take place in a van, with a pipe leading from the van to a shower outlet. This is a service which might well benefit people in Singapore, especially for children or adults who prefer to stay home after the deceased has passed away.

Malaysia

What Malaysia has, as do many other countries, but Singapore does not, is land. When visitors from these countries come to observe Singapore's funeral practices, they are most astonished to see several funeral companies operating and competing side by side at Death Alley. They are more used to stand-alone funeral companies or parlors without any competitors nearby.

Malaysia has space for memorial gardens, which are far more aesthetically pleasing than the cramped cemeteries here. The gardens are places of serene beauty with mounds, streams, pagodas, pavilions, and quaint bridges. Scattered around these memorial gardens are tombstones as well as huge family plots, which are "booked" in advance for the remains of an entire family and those of their descendants.

Unlike in Singapore, where most funeral service providers have to rent their premises from the government at designated locations, a funeral service provider in Malaysia can own an entire building. One of the Malaysian funeral companies I work closely with is headquartered in a five-story facility in Kuala Lumpur that serves public and corporate needs on top of those of its funeral clients. The lobby of the building, which is meant to be used as a funeral parlor, resembles that of a luxury hotel—it has cavernous halls with high ceilings, paneled walls, and marble floors, and is decorated with chandeliers.

The higher floors of the building are reserved for corporate purposes, housing training auditoriums as well as recreational facilities like a cinema and indoor sports facilities for the staff. Free lunches are provided, and staff can take naps in air-conditioned rooms with mattresses. These companies believe that the staff need to be well taken care of so that they can, in return, care for grieving families.

I was impressed at the impeccable level of service provided. This was in 2009, when most of the funeral workers in Singapore were still wearing white long-sleeved (or short-sleeved) shirts, but their Malaysian counterparts were already clad in full suits with jackets.

A separate wing of the building was meant for the general public, who could attend talks on subjects like grief counseling, and cultural and community events. Beyond funerals, the company is also actively involved in the larger mission of promoting cultural diversity and art.

The Malaysian Chinese are better informed than we are in Singapore about Chinese rituals and rites. While in Malaysia, I witnessed numerous traditional rituals I had never seen before in Singapore, including an interesting one signifying the severing of the earthly relationship where the husband of a dead woman broke a comb in two, kept half, and placed the other half in the casket with his wife.

Canada

Canada, too, is blessed with the abundance of land that allows for vast, beautiful memorial gardens, such as those that I saw in Toronto. There are lush trees with leaves that change color with the seasons, from spring greens to autumn yellows, and are a pleasant respite for anyone who is visiting the gardens. Rather than being buried, caskets are sometimes stored above ground in mausoleums or crypts. This is generally not accepted by the Chinese, who believe that the bodies must be buried (or cremated) for the dead to rest in peace. There is a saying, 入土 为安, *rù tǔ wéi ān*, which means that when one is buried, one is at rest.

For the dead who have been cremated, there are also memorial gardens where cremation urns may be buried at the base of the boulders that have been placed along bridges that span tranquil streams, or nestled in the garden walls.

Funeral facilities are equally expansive. In large, spacious funeral parlors, there are homely areas with plenty of couches for people to sink into. The ladies' restrooms were particularly comfortable, with powder stations. I was told that people sometimes seek privacy and cry in the bathrooms.

I witnessed a funeral where a Canadian family, who were Chinese-Buddhists, were saying goodbye to the family's matriarch and were seated near the cremator. The elderly visitors sat on a couch, while the deceased's children knelt by one side of the casket. The chanting of Buddhist prayers continued as the cremator was heating up. When it reached the required temperature, a green light lit up. Upon seeing the light, the funeral director gently guided the son of the deceased to the button. He said, "When you are ready, you can press it." This is not a practice in Singapore.

The son took an interminably long pause. He rested his head on the wall, the emotional struggle written on his face as he anguished over the last task he had to perform for his mother. The doors to the cremator would have opened and he would have been able to feel the heat of the flames once he pressed the button. In the end, he could not bring himself to do so. Instead, the funeral director pressed the button.

I could not help but ask myself: If I were in the same situation, would I have been able to press that button? When the casket enters the furnace, it is always an emotional moment, as that is when the family knows that the physical presence of their loved one will be gone forever. It is even worse if they have to be the one who has to initiate the process.

In Singapore, while there is no button to press, it is common for people to witness when the casket is pushed into the cremator. As they gather in a glass-fronted viewing hall, crematorium workers on the other side of the glass will do the job of pushing the casket out of the hall.

In the Western countries I have visited, such as Canada, New Zealand, and Australia, most families generally do not want to be present to see the casket going into the incinerator. Thus, when I organize funerals for Westerners in Singapore, I can fully understand why they usually request to skip the viewing hall altogether.

In these countries, therefore, the last stage is conducted quite differently. In Australia, I have seen instances where the funeral director presses a button for a set of curtains to be drawn over the casket, like at the close of a show. Thus, the last thing the visitors will see as they exit the room will be the closing of the curtains. I learned from the funeral celebrant course I took that

Australians are usually given a choice of having closed curtains, opened curtains, or sheer

curtains during the ceremony. But my key takeaway is to give people options. When I had to organize the funeral of a special-needs child who had a seizure while in school and died, the family did not want the casket to be seen at all. In place of where the casket would usually stand, we placed a large photo portrait of the boy instead.

In New Zealand, at some of the funerals that I have witnessed, the casket is lowered into an underground incinerator, but the visitors do not see the full lowering of the casket. When the funeral director pushes a button, the casket descends until only the top is visible. The funeral director then stops the process and invites everyone to head toward the reception area for refreshments, after which the casket is fully lowered to the basement where crematorium workers will deliver it into the cremator, behind the scenes.

Also, instead of a funeral wake, the usual practice in these Western countries is to have what is called a visitation or a viewing. Unlike a wake, where people have several days to pay their respects and say goodbye, a visitation only lasts one to two hours, followed immediately by the funeral. When I was studying to be a funeral celebrant in Australia, I was the only foreigner in the class, and the rest of my Australian classmates were astounded, even appalled, to hear that funeral wakes in Singapore last for an average of five days. "Why would you want the body to be at rest for so long?" they asked. They were puzzled why we should mourn over the death of a loved one for such an extended period.

During the visitation, the deceased will not be in the casket yet. They will be placed on a dressing table, usually in a smaller room, so that visitors can touch and kiss their loved one. Embalming is therefore crucial for visitations, so that the body is sanitized and is safe to touch. An embalmer colleague once said he often has to touch up the makeup of the deceased after visitations, as it would have been smeared. While the practice in Singapore is for wakes to be organized soon after the death, in some countries bodies might be kept for several days until a suitable time for the visitation.

France

French funerary culture is similar to those in Australia and New Zealand. When my mother-in-law passed away at home in 2017 on a Friday evening due to her illness, my husband called me on FaceTime and asked me what he should do. I guided him the same way I would guide any family member of the deceased: wipe her down, place a rolled towel under her chin, and damp cotton wool over her eyelids. I immediately booked my flight and flew into France two days later.

I remember the horror that my father-in-law had to go through when he called for a doctor to certify her death. When the doctor picked up the phone, he replied that it was way past his office hours, and that he would come by the next day at 11 am. This scenario would never happen in Singapore.

The following day, they waited for my brother-in-law to fly in, and went to the only two funeral homes in the town to look at their services. My mother-in-law was only transferred to the one the family had decided on late on Saturday night.

When I arrived, I helped put together a memorial page for her, so that her friends could leave messages for the family. I also took my father-in-law shopping because in their culture, it is important to dress smart for their spouse's funeral, contrary to the culture in Singapore.

Her funeral service was the following Saturday morning, so I asked to do the visitation on a Wednesday. Due to her illness, she had not put on makeup for over six years, so I got her some cosmetics and nail polish, intending to make sure she looked her very best if the embalmer had not done a good job.

She was resting on a dressing table in a small room within the funeral home. Her hair, as expected, was back-combed. I asked for a hair dryer and hairbrush, but apparently the embalming center was not on the same premises. My husband had to head home to retrieve the items. I touched up her makeup and redid her hair so that she looked like how she did before she had gotten ill. When my father-in-law saw her afterwards, he was very pleased, and he jokingly said, "Now, I look older than my wife!" (He is actually four years younger than her.)

The funeral was simple but somber. Everyone was dressed very formally, the gentlemen in their suits. I was glad I could contribute to her final journey this way, so that she may rest in peace forever.

Philippines

In the Philippines, I visited a funeral parlor where a trough for the burning of joss sticks was placed just outside the entrance against the wall, and no joss sticks were allowed inside the parlor. When I returned to Singapore, I followed their example and separated the incense-burning area from our air-conditioned, enclosed funeral parlor to keep out the smoke, which in the past would sting the eyes of visitors and was unbearable for those with respiratory problems.

I met a man in the Philippines who was very eager to talk about his work, which was justifiably noble: he organized funerals for the destitute who died in the streets. But when he led me to the embalming room of his funeral parlor, I was shocked by what I saw. About 20 bodies were laid around the room, and some were stacked one on top of the other. None were in body bags. The stark image made me realize the limited resources with which that gentleman had to work.

The Philippines has the largest Catholic population in Asia. They believe that their loved one returns to God after death, so the element of celebration and commemoration comes across strongly in funerals, which are large, communal events where everyone, friends and family, gets together to celebrate the life of the deceased. There are photos shared, and a lot of food is eaten. For that reason, funeral parlors have kitchens for family members to cook in. Guests may also bring food along as if the funeral were a potluck.

The family mausoleums I saw in the Philippines, located in the memorial gardens, were also the biggest I have ever seen. These are huge plots, larger than houses, bought by wealthy Filipinos for themselves and their descendants. Some resemble terrace houses, all in a row, and may be lavishly fitted out with chandeliers and gold ceilings.

Even more interesting is how external caretakers are paid to stay in these mausoleums, which have kitchens and servants' quarters along with the crypts that house the caskets and bodies. While living alongside the dead, the caretaker's job is to guard valuables, do some gardening, clean the mausoleum, and maintain the condition of the space. The arrangement benefits both the families of the dead and those of the caretakers, and also alleviates housing shortages and rising population.

On All Saints' Day, which is the equivalent of the Qingming Festival in Singapore, when the people pay respects to their dead, these caretakers temporarily move out. All Saints' Day is a spectacle in itself, as the usually silent graveyards become venues of festivity and parties. The Filipinos clean their loved ones' graves, decorate them, stay overnight in the cemetery, eat, sing karaoke, and even dance, amid a sea of candles and lights.

In some instances, the cemeteries evolve into living villages that provide the poor with a place to stay among the dead, complete with shops selling all manner of sundries.

China

China is the obvious home of traditional Chinese funeral practices, but during my visits to China, I also found some of them to be surprisingly progressive.

For instance, the traditional requirement for family members to pin on their shirt sleeve a fabric square has been modified to something more straightforward and elegant. I saw how family members all wore a black heart-shaped badge with just the word 孝, *xiào* (filial piety), on it, instead of fabric squares based on a complex color code, while guests wore white roses pinned to their shirts.

It was also in China where I saw a decedent care spa, an idea that the particular funeral practitioner had modified from Japanese funeral practices, where family members can witness and participate in preparing and pampering the body—which has already been embalmed—before it is placed in the casket. Usually, this is done behind closed doors. I felt that involving the family members in the process could help them feel closer to the deceased. They could also feel assured that the deceased is being given tender loving care on the last leg of their life journey.

The procedure is fairly formal in tone—two care therapists, masked and gowned, give the deceased a head and facial massage, moisturize his skin, buff his nails, and shave his beard (if he is usually clean-shaven in life). It is like a spa treatment. They precede each action with a formal recitation in Mandarin of what they will be doing, and the family members of the deceased will be invited at some point to go through the gesture of wiping the deceased's face, hands, and feet to express their filial piety.

Hong Kong

Like Singapore, Hong Kong is a city that is land-starved and is confronting an aging population, which results in an increasing number of deaths every year. However, the funeral situation there is more dire than the one in Singapore.

When someone dies, he has to wait in a queue for a cremation slot. These precious slots are usually booked a month or two in advance, and in the meantime, the body is kept in cold storage. Embalming is generally not done. When the grandmother of a friend from Hong Kong died, I was very concerned and asked if he would be flying back home immediately. He replied matter of factly that he would only set off in two months, as that was when the cremation would be held.

After the cremation, the queuing continues. Columbarium facilities where cremains can be stored are full to bursting. A funeral director quoted in a 2015 China Daily report estimated that there are between 80,000 and 100,000 urns containing cremains scattered around Hong Kong, which are in storage in private homes or funeral homes until a permanent niche becomes available.

The challenges in building new storage facilities are exacerbated by the fact that the superstitious Chinese in Hong Kong—just like those in Singapore—do not want the remains of the dead near where they live as it drives down property prices. The Hong Kong government is now contemplating the possibility of building columbariums in nearby mainland China or Macau.

It was also in Hong Kong at a funeral conference where I saw a professional, whom I would call an artist, whose medium is human bones. When a grave is exhumed, the bones of the person who was previously buried are picked out and laid out. He then carefully places the bones in a set crisscross manner into an urn, such that they "lock" onto each other. The last piece that goes into the urn is the skull. His arrangement is so precise that even if the urn were turned on its side and rolled around, the bones would not budge. I reckon he has a busy schedule, given that the government has been forced to dig up the dead every six years to free up valuable burial space.

Nepal

Nepal is a deeply spiritual country where Buddhists co-exist with Hindus, and where people gather for picnics or a day out in the local park to watch public cremations.

Such cremations are carried out every day at the Pashupatinath Temple, a grand Hindu temple that is also the largest Hindu crematorium in Kathmandu. Bodies wrapped in white and orange cloth are carried to the edge of the Bagmati River, which runs alongside the temple, to be cleansed and prepared for cremation. On the other side of the narrow river is a hill where people—even tourists—can gather to watch the proceedings. For most people, who have previously only glimpsed dead strangers in passing hearses, the openness and accessibility of this cremation site are truly unique.

Once prepared, the body is covered up, laid on a funeral pyre consisting of wooden logs stacked in a crisscross manner on a platform, and set alight. A row of over 10 platforms line the river. The cremains are then swept into the river.

Although waxy feet and parts of the body are occasionally visible during the entire process, there is an air of serenity amongst the spectators. Apart from the tourists, who snap away madly with their cameras, the locals enjoy the trees and the scenery while munching on snacks, seeming to accept that death is truly just part of life.

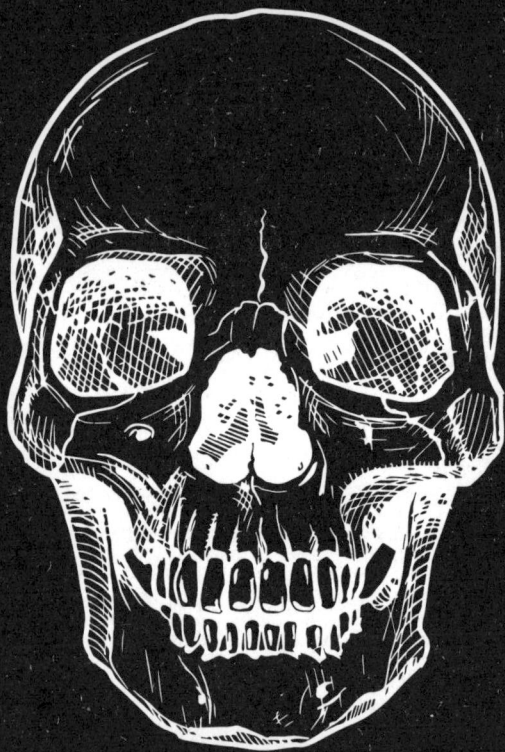

CHAPTER 15

Preparing for the End

I am now 39, and I'm perfectly healthy. However, I drew up my first will at the age of 24. I also redrew my will after giving birth to my baby girl.

I have invested in sufficient insurance protection to ensure that my family will not have to deal with frightening hospital bills or pay the mortgage on my apartment and other costs when I die. I have also planned my funeral, so all of my staff know exactly what to do in the event of my death.

There are so many life stages that we plan carefully for and splurge on. We save up for the perfect wedding, the dream honeymoon, the baby's lavish first month celebration, milestone anniversaries, and birthday parties. So it's odd that while each of us is given an entire lifetime to plan for our funerals and what happens after our deaths, most people don't—not even some funeral directors. I've heard excuses such as having no time, being unable to bring themselves to do what they feel is depressing, or not wanting to plan for something that they themselves cannot enjoy.

I have come across many cases of sudden death. My beloved uncle, the youngest brother of my father, died unexpectedly of a heart attack in February 2018. He was just 60 years old. He had arrived at the ferry terminal, had gone to the toilet, and as he was about to walk out, he gripped at his heart and collapsed. Medics rushed to the site and tried to revive him, but he was pronounced dead at the hospital after a few hours.

He rejected a heart bypass surgery he was recommended to do several years ago because he was afraid that if he required post-surgery care, he would have no one to rely on. He was a bachelor. I wish he had gone for it, because I really miss him.

During my first year in the funeral business, I attended to a death caused by acute myocardial infarction. This was a man in his eighties who had keeled over and died suddenly after a chicken rice dinner with his family at a famous stall along Thomson Road. A doctor from a nearby clinic certified that the elderly man was dead, and when the family asked him if he knew of any funeral directors, the doctor suggested that they call me. I was then at home relaxing after dinner, but upon receiving the call, I rushed down to the Care Center with my mother to meet the family there.

The family had driven over with the old man's body propped up in the car, as if he were a passenger. When I approached them, they looked frantic and were not quite able to accept what had just happened. I quickly offered a helping hand and, with the assistance of my staff, lifted the gentleman out of the car, moved him into the Care Center, and laid him out on the embalming table. His wife wailed for hours, scolding him for leaving her so soon. We waited for her and the rest of the family to calm down and compose themselves before embarking on discussions about the funeral, which ended at about midnight, as they often broke down in tears.

A friend of mine, whom I used to see often at salsa social nights, moved to Hawaii. To my great horror, the next time I heard about her, it was that she had been shot dead there by her American fiancé. All I could think of was the last conversation we had had before she moved.

Then there was the man in his thirties who died in his sleep. That was the only occasion where I witnessed an actual moment of death via a CCTV recording. The person who died was a man with special needs. His mother was a client who became a friend of mine, and at the time he died, good things were happening in his life as he was going to start school at Movement for the Intellectually Disabled of Singapore. In Singapore, MINDS is the first school that focuses on students with autism. But on National Day 2018, my friend suddenly called me at 7 am, frantic, to tell me she found him in bed that morning, dead. After combing through the CCTV footage, which recorded what happened in the room for her to keep tabs on his safety, I saw the moment when he died. He had been lying, peacefully asleep for all appearances, when he appeared to have a seizure, and then he stopped moving moments later. There and then, I saw someone take his last breath. It was a sobering experience.

It is important to me that, even if I were to die suddenly, my loved ones would be spared the hassle of having to deal with the aftermath. Therefore, to those who say that dying in their sleep is the best way to go, I would respond that it is only if they have planned their funerals and made provisions for their families.

My conviction stems from what my family and I had to deal with after my father's death. We were emotionally overwrought and sleep-deprived, having kept vigil at the hospital over the last few days and nights. None of us had any idea what kind of funeral he would have wanted. We even had difficulty finding a photograph that would be used for his wake and funeral, to place on the altar, because he was too busy in his life to have solo photographs taken of himself. Family photographs with him in them were scarce. He also didn't write a will or buy any insurance, and the $8,752 he had left in the bank was money that we could not get our hands on until two years after his death, when all the paperwork had been sorted out.

There are a few components to think of in death planning: signing the Advance Medical Directive (AMD), having a Lasting Power of Attorney (LPA) in place, making a will, buying insurance coverage, and pre-planning for the funeral itself. Thanks to efforts by groups like the Lien Foundation, which champions end-of-life awareness, as well as government campaigns, more people in Singapore are writing wills and making decisions concerning not just their funerals, but also how they want to die.

The AMD is a legal document that you sign in advance to inform your doctor that you do not want the use of any life-sustaining treatments to prolong your life in the event you become terminally ill, unconscious, or when death is imminent. There is also the LPA, another legal document, which allows a person to appoint an individual to make key decisions for him, should he lose his mental capacity and become unable to do so on his own. The government strongly recommends that Singaporeans sign the LPA. I told myself after Pa passed away that I would not be a burden to my family. I completed my LPA in 2016 because we never know when we might lose our mental capacity due to accident or illness.

According to a *Straits Times* report in 2014, over 2,500 people applied for the LPA between April 2013 and March 2014, compared to 655 people who did so in the same timeframe three years earlier. This is due to increasing awareness of the existence of such a document, as well as moves by the Singapore government to encourage people to apply for one, including waiving application fees and simplifying the forms.

There has also been an increasing awareness about the AMD. About 1,800 people signed the AMD in 2013, up from about 500 a decade ago.

Financial planning, especially for those who have others depending on them, is crucial.

I knew of a man in his mid-thirties who died of leukemia and left behind his wife, who had stopped work to take care of him and their 11-year-old child. The family had to borrow $200,000 to pay the medical bills he had incurred during the two years he was ill. He had not expected that he would fall so sick and had not bought an insurance plan that covered all his medical expenses.

Many people fall sick unexpectedly or die suddenly and do not have adequate insurance coverage or savings. They would rather spend the money on things they can enjoy, as they think that it is very unlikely that they will fall gravely ill. And even if they did, they would rather use their disposable income to pay their medical bills. But all we need is just one "what if" to come true, and it could wipe out whatever money they had saved from not buying medical insurance. They could very well leave their family members in debt from having to pay their hospital bills.

As for funeral pre-planning, there are a growing number of people worldwide who are doing so. In the United Kingdom, the first funeral plan was launched in 1986. Since then, one of its leading funeral plan providers, Dignity, has helped more than 600,000 people make advance provisions for their funerals. The numbers are growing every year—more than 135,000 people in the UK made provisions in 2013—to protect against rising funeral costs, to leave money behind for loved ones, and to take care of the details of the funeral in advance.

In Australia, funeral planning provisions are also in place. People can plan and pay for their funerals in advance, or invest in funeral bonds that can be paid to a funeral director when they pass on. In a 2015 article in the *Australian Financial Review*, a funeral director said, "People can choose the type of service they want: the coffin or casket, minister or celebrant, cremation or burial."

In the smartphone and tablet era, there are death apps with which people can plan their own funerals. These promise to help people organize an after-death package of digital living wills, funeral plans, multimedia memorial portfolios, and digital estate arrangements.

In Singapore, those who pre-plan their funerals are usually people who have experienced a health scare and were forced to think about their own mortality. They might have seen how the lack of funeral planning can affect those left behind. They could also be already suffering from terminal illnesses like cancer, AIDS, or kidney diseases. Chronic death, unlike acute death, is predictable. The silver lining for those suffering from terminal illnesses is that they have time to prepare for death: to complete bucket lists, say their goodbyes in meaningful ways, and put their affairs in order.

Most of the time, it's those who are already dying who are prepared to talk about death. One of my clients was a French woman, a former teacher, who lived in Singapore with her son. She was frail and sickly, had to go around with an oxygen tank, and she was convinced that she would die soon. I met her five times to discuss her funeral preparations. She was alone, for her son was not ready to join in the conversation about her impending death. She spoke only French and broken English. With the help of my husband as translator, we met at her home surreptitiously, when her son was not there. She was so ill that she was always clad in her nightgown, but she was very focused and made it clear what she wanted.

As she was too frail to travel, she would probably not be able to return to Paris to die. She did not want to have a wake. She chose the clothes that she wanted to wear in the casket and packed them in a bag. She selected the songs to be played at her funeral and the poems to be read out. She wanted to make a voice recording to be broadcast during her funeral, so I arranged for a professional soundman to go to her residence. She approved the design of the funeral booklet and stipulated that five bottles of champagne were to be set aside for her guests. She wanted her son to bring her cremains back to Paris to scatter in a specific garden, and she even chose the design of the urn. Once she had talked through and was happy with all of her decisions, she paid for the entire funeral.

When she dies, her domestic helper has been directed to extract the folder containing all of her instructions, as well as the clothes she has chosen, and let her son know of her decisions.

Sometimes, those who are dying try to get their family members involved in the discussion. If the deceased's wishes are known in advance, it will spare the family members from having to deal with the hostility and conflict that might arise from arguments over what the deceased would have preferred. They would be free to grieve for the deceased in peace.

At the hospices I work with, the staff often encounter dying patients who are ready to talk about their funerals, and they have to gently guide the family members who may not be quite so ready. While this might be a difficult conversation to have, such discussions ultimately pave the way for calm, ordered funerals that proceed smoothly because the deceased had made his wishes known ahead of time.

A gentleman once came to me to arrange his funeral. He was thin from having suffered from cancer for five years. He had a long beard, the sort that Taoist priests of old would have had, but what struck me was his incredibly calm demeanor and acceptance of his impending demise. In all our discussions about his funeral, conducted in his beautifully spoken Mandarin, he was completely calm, never upset, angry, nor conflicted.

He usually came with two of his three sons, who earnestly and dutifully took notes. He told them that he did not want a wake as he did not have many close friends. He did not wish to be embalmed, but wanted a simple, short funeral followed by a straight cremation. He also did not want to wear shoes while he was in the casket, for he felt that as he was born without shoes, he should leave the same way. He even cracked a joke, which I remember: "But I will have to wear clothes, won't I?"

Sometimes, his sons asked questions. "Who do you want us to contact when you die, Pa?" He gave them a list that comprised close relatives.

On one occasion, his eldest son also came. As I repeated the decisions that the old man had made during our first few meetings, it was clear that this son was finding it very hard to talk about his father's death.

The greatest contention arose when the gentleman said that he wished for his cremains to be scattered anywhere, as long as it was amongst nature. I explained to him that the scattering of remains is permanent and irretrievable, and is not an option I generally recommend. But he smiled and said he knew what he wanted. "I want to return to nature," he said. His three sons looked at one another. The younger two eventually nodded, albeit somewhat reluctantly, but the eldest was still disturbed. He asked his father, "Is this what you really want?"

The gentleman said, "You don't have to remember me by my cremains. Look inside your heart—that is how you will remember me."

Four months later, he died at home, as was his wish. His quiet funeral, which was attended by a small group of fewer than 10, went exactly the way he had requested, and his remains were scattered.

I, too, have planned my own funeral. I have already informed my husband that if I should die before he does, he is to be in charge of my cremains and can decide on my behalf what is to be done with them. I just ask that my remains are close to his, hopefully in a sacred space where I had made many beautiful memories with him. I have designated my own funeral staff to take charge of specific tasks, and they know exactly who has to do what, as I have made all the decisions.

The funeral will be a joyful, exuberant celebration of all that I treasure. I will have my hair down, have my nails painted red, and I will be clad in my favorite lime green *cheongsam* dress. When I told my family this, my sister Sarah, who is an embalmer and will be embalming me, quipped, "What if you can't fit into the cheongsam? Shall I cut the back?" Red roses will decorate my casket while my collection of fans will be prominently displayed. In my white casket will be placed my dancing boots, my Ray-Ban sunglasses, and more of my fans. No one will wear black because I do not want my funeral to be a sad event. Moreover, I have been wearing black almost all the time because of my work, and it would be nice for my send-off to feature colorful outfits and music. There will be a karaoke machine for guests to dedicate songs to me, and preferably a temporary dance floor at my funeral wake where people can come and dance to Latin music. I am also thinking of a memorial service at my favorite salsa club in Clarke Quay and a live band playing the Latin music I love, such as salsa, kizomba, bachata, chacha, merengue, and tango, so that all who attend will remember me that way.

I have already started a memorial website, which I constantly update with photos, videos, and messages that I would like to share with my loved ones. I have been using this website since 2015 to record my thoughts, final wishes, letters to my loved ones, and videos that I would like them to watch. I was actually inspired by the movie *P.S. I Love You*, where the protagonist, played by Gerard Butler, arranges a beautiful post-funeral journey for his wife so that she can move on after his death. What I saw in the movie drove me to plan my own funeral and the way I would like to be remembered.

I have had fun thinking about all these details, which will change as my life goes on. organizing your own funeral should not be a sad, dreary affair. It can be a joyful one, especially if you are doing it while you are still healthy. We cannot decide how we come into this earth, but we have a whole lifetime to think about how we want our funerals to be when we leave. I want my funeral to be a lifetime in a day.

In Bhutan, which has been called the happiest country on earth, its people are expected to think about their own deaths five times a day. A 2015 BBC article on this practice, which tried to draw an explanation for the apparent disconnect between happiness and death, quoted a research study: "Death is a psychologically threatening fact, but when people contemplate it, apparently the automatic system begins to search for happy thoughts."

Bestselling author Stephen Covey, in *The 7 Habits of Highly Effective People*, also advocates that you think about your funeral. The second habit—"Begin with the End in Mind"—suggests that you visualize your own funeral: Who will be there? What will people say about how you lived your life? What sort of relationships did you have? How would your priorities change if you had only 30 more days to live?

Planning for your funeral can change your life and your legacy.

CHAPTER 16

Life Lessons

*T*love my mother, but it wasn't until I witnessed a life-changing funeral that I realized how important it was for us both that she knew this.

The funeral took place in Auckland, New Zealand. At the end of the service for an old lady, the guests were asked to leave the chapel after each had placed a rose on the casket. I noticed a teenage girl, clad in jeans, with long, chestnut-brown hair, sitting alone in the fourth row of the pews. Once the chapel had emptied, she came to us and asked if we could open the casket, which we did. She then asked for some time alone with the deceased who, as we found out, was her grandmother. We left the chapel, but over the CCTV, we witnessed the girl crying and apologizing to her grandmother for the quarrel they had had just before she had died.

I had argued with my mother in the past over business-related decisions. When she had said something I had not agreed with, I had retaliated strongly. But what I saw in New Zealand caused me to realize that if either of us should die unexpectedly, the last thing we would want is to leave each other on bad terms.

I decided to stop fighting with my mother. If I got angry, I talked to her only after I had calmed down and sent her text messages to apologize. I started hugging her and telling her I love her, which was previously unheard of in our emotionally undemonstrative traditional Chinese family.

There are many ways in which my job has transformed the way I live my life—some of the biggest changes are how I have learned not to take my loved ones for granted, and I now put much greater effort into healing relationship rifts.

Other than the Auckland funeral, there have been too many occasions during which I have seen how people are burdened by regrets from bad relationships. As we go through life, there are those whom we will love, but unavoidably others whom we will hate. There are people who will offend us, make our lives miserable, or commit what we might deem are unforgivable acts against us. The grudges that we bear are emotional burdens that weigh heavily on our hearts—sometimes even against our own family members. Dad was a lousy father; Mum never loved me—why should I forgive them?

But death changes all that. Often, the finality of death and the loss of any future chance at reconciliation suddenly break down the emotional walls that were put up to guard against pain. There are instances in which the deceased might, sometimes for decades, have had to live with being resented or ignored. Being hated by a loved one while you are on your deathbed does not make for a peaceful death.

I have seen visitors—sometimes even family members—say at funerals that they are sorry for not having apologized to the deceased while they were still alive. Funerals are when these regrets are laid bare. As people cry their way through litanies of "I should have" or "I shouldn't have," I often wonder, why didn't you tell that to the deceased when they were alive?

I rely on four phrases that I believe to be the bedrock of reconciliation, and that guide me every day in how I treat my loved ones, from my mother to my family members to my husband: "I'm sorry"; "Please forgive me"; "I thank you"; "I love you." These originate from Joe Vitale in his book, *Zero Limits*, who explains that these four simple sentences about forgiveness are based on a Hawaiian healing technique known as *Ho'opono'pono*, which dates back thousands of years and literally translates to "make right" or "to restore balance."

We also tend not to use these phrases with the people who matter most. At an exhibition about funerals and preparing for death, I held a discussion with a group of youths. The subject was on how we can say "I love you" in different ways. Every single one of them thought of the phrase in the context of their girlfriends or boyfriends. I asked, "Have any of you thought about saying it to your parents? The first person you think of is one whom you are dating, but the people who take care of you, feed you, and clothe you are ironically the ones whom you take most for granted. And it is when they die that you will regret most not telling them that you love them."

The Chinese, who are notably emotionally reticent and undemonstrative, might find it difficult to verbalize their emotions. Some prefer to show, rather than tell, like my father did. Towards the end of my grandmother's life, I knew he regretted not having taken better care of his mother earlier. He then expressed his love by buying her whatever she needed to make her remaining days more comfortable.

While I make an effort to ensure that my loved ones know that I care for them, I also want to make my life count, and not just in ways that will make for an impressive, long resume. The most meaningful and touching funerals are those where visitors are genuinely grieving because the deceased had touched their lives in some way. They might have lent a listening ear to someone whom no one else would listen to, quietly helped a friend or colleague without fanfare, or encouraged someone in their darkest hour.

In this regard, I hope to be able to measure up to my father. Over a decade has passed since his death, but people still tell me stories about what he did for them. He found great joy in giving money to those who needed it more than he did—he kept a stack of red packets[10] in the glove compartment of his car that he doled out to the elderly chefs of restaurants he ate at. He also gave generously to hospices, charitable organizations, and senior citizens' homes, and participated actively in their events.

Sometimes, stories like these, of those who have passed away, only emerge during their wakes. A young man whom no one recognized attended the funeral of an old lady that I had organized. The visitor told her family that he had met the old lady at a hawker center[11] when he had mistaken her for a destitute elderly person and had offered her money to buy food, as she was drinking just water. She retorted, "Young man, I'm thirsty—I'm not hungry or poor." They began chatting and subsequently struck up a friendship—it was one that saved his life as he later confessed to her that his wife had died and he was contemplating suicide. The old lady talked him out of it. While his story made the old lady's family cry, it also put a smile on their faces when they realized the size of the legacy she had left behind, even to a complete stranger.

Making a difference is not limited by one's age. When I organized a memorial service for a 15-year-old girl who had died from a brain aneurysm, more than a hundred people turned up, and it was apparent that she was well-loved. Her school principal, teachers, and friends waxed lyrical about her drive to help others, which had led her to volunteer with an organization that helped unemployed people to find jobs.

---

10 The small red envelopes in which gifts of money are given on special occasions.
11 A Singaporean food cart pod.

My thinking towards life and how I want to approach it has changed too. When or how I die is clearly beyond my control and I'm not really afraid of dying—what I do fear is not living my life to the fullest before my time is up. I live by my motto: Live with no regrets. Leave with no regrets.

In the past, I would have had reservations and doubts before embarking on anything new. These days, in my work and in my personal life, I venture forth. I wanted to write a book; I want to start a school to provide training in professional funeral services; I want to transform how funerals are conducted in Singapore.

There will be criticism from naysayers and competitors in the industry. When we first introduced Showers of Love, the service was deemed inappropriate by some funeral service directors. But, apart from what my clients say, I have learned not to let the opinions of others affect or bother me.

Meditation, which I started to do in 2007, helps me to be at peace with myself; I have learned to respond, not react. And I am still constantly learning to be more self-aware. Outside of work, my life is full. I took up salsa dancing the year my father died in 2004 and I do so without inhibitions, even travelling to other countries to dance up a storm with fellow lovers of salsa from around the world. I am further developing my love for learning by constantly trying new experiences, and I am also learning French. Now that I am a mother, I make time to bond with my baby girl even when I am busy. Sometimes, I am unable to see her because I am out of the house before she wakes up and I only return home after she has gone to sleep, but on those days when I can, I bring her out to exercise with me.

In a way, being a funeral director has not only taught me about life; it has empowered me to live the life I want to live. Death is the master of my life.

Don't just add days to your life, add life to your days.

Acknowledgements

My heartfelt thanks go out to all who have helped me make this book a reality:

Lee Poh Hwa, from the Lien Foundation, who heard my stories, saw a glimmer of book potential and referred me to a publisher; Edmund Wee, the CEO of Epigram Books, who took up the gauntlet and said, "Let's do it"; Wong Sher Maine, who gamely took on writing about the death industry, articulating my thoughts, and documenting my memories; Julia Tan, my editor, for her valuable input in polishing up the manuscript.

I also want to thank all my loved ones who have made me who I am today: My beloved Pa, my idol, on whose name I ride, whose name motivates me, and in whose name I find comfort; My super-talented Mum, who is my inspiration. She is one tough woman who shouldered all the family's burdens while taking great care of us; who relentlessly tried to push me away from this tough industry, yet continued to protect, guide, and assist me when I made my choice. I would not be who I am without her; My sisters and brother, Jia Jia, Sarah, and Zachary. I am so blessed to be their sibling. No matter what happens, I know we will always have each others' backs. To them, I want to say, "Thank you for being my forever friends! I miss our Subarashii days!" My granny, who showers me with unconditional love; who was worried I would be kidnapped just like the heroines in her favorite drama serials after seeing me on TV and feared that I would attract attention; who is ever so thrilled to introduce me to wet market stallholders and her friends; and who always nags me to sleep early and eat properly; The rest of my big family, who have always been supportive of the work that I do; My life partner, Emmanuel Jacomy, 易桀明, who has changed my life for the better. He is just as competitive as I am, shares all my interests and complements me wonderfully. Thank you for embracing me for who I am, despite the work that I do. Thank you for giving me the gift of a family now. I am imperfect, but I am grateful that we have both learned to love each other perfectly.

To my baby Eliane Lea. You complete me. You inspire me to become a better, stronger and wiser version of my old self. Thank you for topping up the joy of life in my days.

I am sorry.
Please forgive me.
I thank you.
I love you.

About the Author

ANGJOLIE MEI, formerly a financial advisor, is a certified funeral celebrant and certified funeral director at The Life Celebrant, a provider of boutique funeral services. She is one of the few women in the funeral services industry in Singapore and provides fascinating insights into this little-known profession. This is the second edition of her first book, which has also been translated into Chinese (爱的告别).

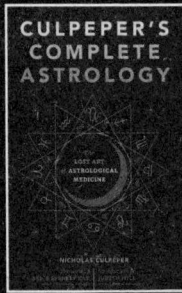